Joanne McNeil (Editor)

Best of
Rhizome
2012

Joanne McNeil (Edited by)
Best of Rhizome 2012

Publisher: LINK Editions, Brescia 2013
www.linkartcenter.eu

Printed and distributed by: Lulu.com
www.lulu.com

ISBN 978-1-291-32991-9

Rhizome is dedicated to the creation, presentation, preservation, and critique of emerging artistic practices that engage technology. Through open platforms for exchange and collaboration, its website serves to encourage and expand the communities around these practices.
Its programs, many of which happen online, include commissions, exhibitions, events, discussion, archives and portfolios.
It supports artists working at the furthest reaches of technological experimentation as well as those responding to the broader aesthetic and political implications of new tools and media. Its organizational voice draws attention to artists, their work, their perspectives and the complex interrelationships between technology, art and culture.
http://rhizome.org/

"[...] the products that come from the ether carry with them the logic of their native territory, as they transit from digital artifact to real world object. The online territory provides a unique mutability, a blend of fictions with reality."

_ JOANNE MCNEIL

Contents

Foreword

Rhizome is an arts organization born of the internet. Since 1996, we have supported contemporary art engaged with technology through a number of programs, many of which happen online.

Our editorial program has become one of our most visible and significant activities. Every day, thousands of people come to the Rhizome website to understand, and question, the role of technology in culture through the writing we publish there. Rhizome's mission and ethos leads our editorial focus – to examine the social, political and aesthetic implications of new technologies, from the perspective of art.

The Best of 2012 is not just a best of Rhizome's work, but a portrait of the year that we hope will gain significance over time for its contextualization and articulation of artists' practices. Artists are predictors and barometers of change, and sensitive to their cultural surroundings. From texts on production in the digital age, to the influence of the Occupy Movement, from drones and surveillance, to online vernacular – these collected essays give a sense of what was informing artists' work, and by extension culture, in 2012.

For all those with stuffed RSS readers, fast-moving Twitter feeds and bookmark pages they never quite return to, we're pleased to see these essays collected into a new format, with a new excuse to read. With thanks to editor Joanne McNeil, all of the writers, Domenico Quaranta and, most importantly, the readers and community surrounding http://www.rhizome.org.

Heather Corcoran
Executive Director, Rhizome

2

Orit Gat

Screen. Image. Text.

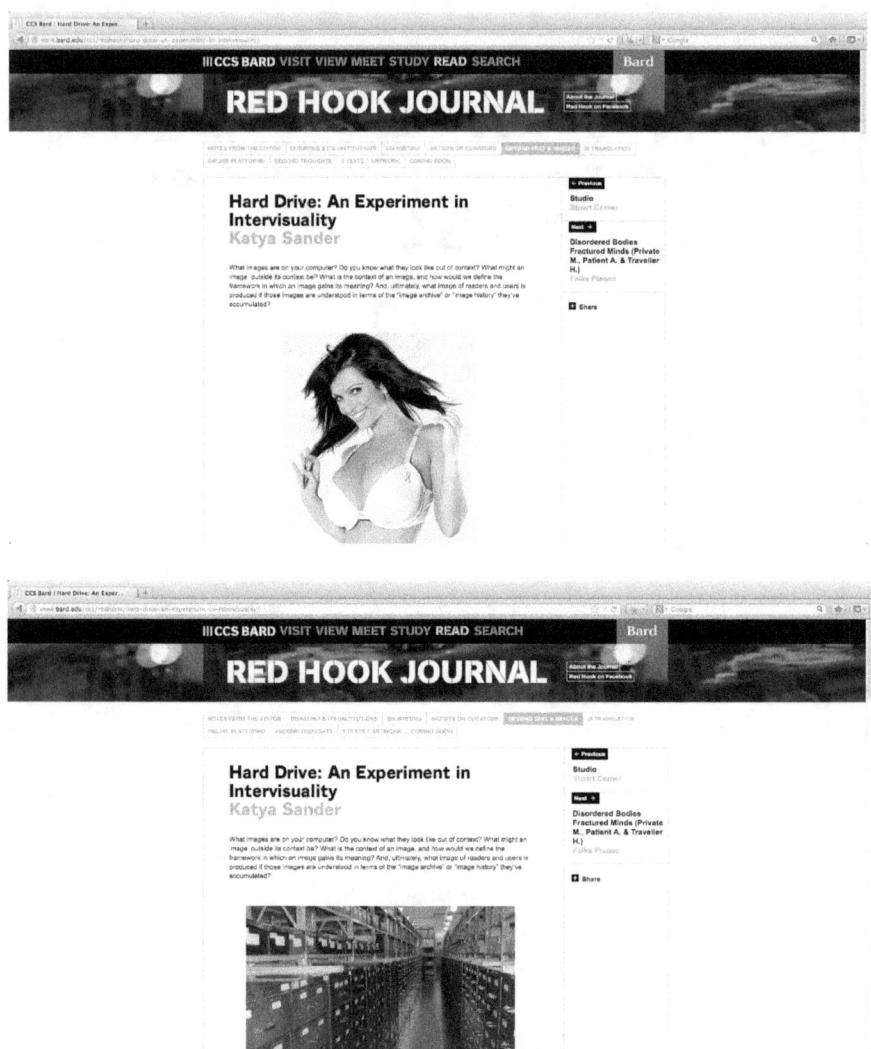

Two screenshots of Katya Sander's online project *Hard Drive*, 2011

I once heard Leon Botstein, the President of Bard College, compare books to stairs. "They've invented the elevator," he said, "but sometimes you still walk up." There are countless discussions on the future of the book – they are picked up in magazine feature articles, in trade conferences, and in academic roundtables – and in all of these, the future of the printed word seems certain: in a generation or two, print will become obsolete. In this age of changing habits, if print is the stairs and screens the elevator, then what could the escalator be?

This moment in time, and the awareness of the possibilities electronic publishing grants, affect the manner in which we relate to texts in a way that is under constant scrutiny. But images prove to be a different problem. The separation between text and images has a long history. In fact, images have posed a challenge for publishers from the early days of print – be it the cost of printing them; the payments for illustrators, photographers, and designers; or simply contextualizing the images and their relation to the text – but they have become crucial to our understanding of texts. When the *Illustrated London News*, the world's first illustrated weekly newspaper, began publishing in 1842, the relationship between the text and the engraved images in the paper was such a novelty that it took the weekly about a decade to stake a hold in that era's news distribution channels. Once it did, it became one of the most widely circulated newspapers in Victorian Britain. The marriage of text and the engraved image marked a new level of fluency in communication via images, which does away with staples of early print day, even though the separation between image and text lasted for many decades later, and can still be traced today. (Think, for example, of the plate pages, where color images were glued onto the paper, so that the book or magazine would be printed in black and white, adding the color pages later in a way that saves money on printing, but also generates a wholly different relationship with images. These are often associated with encyclopedias, but a large number of artist's monographs retained this design even after color printing became widely accessible, creating the odd text-image relationship where an artwork is described to the most minute detail, with a comment in parenthesis directing the reader to "color plate 3," where the mentioned piece could be seen in glossy print.)

The generations to come of age in the days of digital publishing and reading on screens have a much more complicated relationship with images. The human eye-brain system is capable of reading a large number of high quality images in a matter of split seconds, and this, alongside the hand-eye coordination – think about the pleasure of a touch screen versus inky newspaper pages – is rapidly developing to mirror our changing habits of consuming information. So much so that the contemporary heightened sensitivity to the way we read images can lead to an ability to, at times, ignore the quality of the images when inserted into a text, the way our brain glides over a typo in the flow of reading. The way we read images online is only one thing these magazines deal with in the process of publishing, but it is surely an element that dictates a large part of the reading experience of these publications.

The endless discussions on the future of print bring up the contemporary fluency with images on a regular basis. Aside from the fact that digital publishing is often cheaper and always easier to disseminate, many consider the role of the image in digital publishing to be a key aspect in the contemporary experience of reading. The benefits of handheld devices are considered time and again, especially in relation to embedding a variety of image formats: slideshows, moving images, animated GIFs, and so forth. A number of start-ups like Flyp bring screen-based reading beyond the initial technology, and enhanced e-books are quite widely considered to be the next major option offered by electronic reading devices.

Whereas some of the aforementioned key possibilities that publishing online presents may seem so pertinent to contemporary art publishing, they also bring up a number of crucial issues in the relationship between the screen, the text, and the image. In the past few years, contemporary art publishing has had to somehow consider all of these questions – be it print publications that have to strategize their web presence or online publications that need to carve out a place for themselves in the web's infinite possibilities for distraction. Taking into consideration a number of web-based contemporary art magazines, I asked editors to answer a number of questions about the way their editorial lines react to the possibilities and restrictions of the internet environment. Questions considered things like what online distribution offered, the economies of attention on the internet, sourcing images online, and finally, the relationship between print and web-based media, especially considering current tendencies of online art publications to come out with print readers.

Distribution: The Internet's Nuts and Bolts

"Intention follows a platform that you can deal with and afford," says *Mousse*'s Head of Publications Stefano Cernuschi. *Mousse* [1] is printed in newspaper form, but also has extensive online presence and recently launched a dedicated iPad app. The distribution of print publications follows certain sets of rules – perfect binding, for example, helps – and a number of print publications utilize the internet as another distribution platform. *Artforum* and *Frieze*, for instance, upload each issue's table of contents but only make a number of articles available online for free, thus enticing readers to buy the print magazine. *Frieze* uploads all older content, whereas *Artforum* has a unique website too, which includes web-only features like certain reviews and the infamous Diary section.

At the early days of the internet, users became accustomed to getting things for free, content especially, but once the first popular sites introduced paywalls, many followed and many will trail. Online magazine *Triple Canopy* [2] recently introduced a membership system, asking its readers for $3 a month; the magazine will still be freely accessible to non-members, but a system of remuneration is indeed being considered, a complex idea based on a notion of community: that readers will pay for what they can get for free because they would like to support the magazine.

So what about Cernuschi's "platform you can afford"? Clearly, publishing online comes to a fraction of the printing costs, which is one of the obvious reasons to go online. Another is distribution. While going viral on the internet is still a process that is a mystery to many (not to mention the example of the somewhat unexpected online popularity of cats), web readership, even if murky and somewhat untrackable really, can be a constant surprise that is inexistent in a print magazine, even when considering the idea that a print product might circulate between more than the one person who pays for it at a given store. And with online readership comes the new idea of participation. In "The Journey West," his editorial and declaration of intent, Thomas Lawson, the Editor-in-Chief of Los Angeles-based online magazine *East of Borneo* [3], explains that the magazine's "genesis has been long and deliberative: several years of thinking past the delights and constraints of the printed page, and one very intense year of thinking through the actual possibilities of current online publication." [4] One of the publication's stated intents is to build up an ongoing archive about Los Angeles and its cultural scene, and one way *East of Borneo* found to do this is incorporate its readers. Thus, readers can upload content to the site, contribute texts and source material, and partake in the construction of the site as a resource. These examples take the idea of the dated notion of web 2.0 user-generated content to a level different than Facebook, to use the obvious example. While Facebook makes its users work for it, they do not partake in a larger Facebook community (in fact, the social network parcels out users' sense of community for them: a school attended, a workplace, etc.). What these publications do is harness the user-generated labor and value (monetary or cultural) in order to create a sense of public.

What We Pay for Attention

The internet gets confusing at times. We consume enormous amounts of information online, the origins of which we often can't point to, except for in our browser's history. Publishing online seems like such an obvious choice – it's cheap, widely accessible, and so "of our time," to paraphrase Baudelaire's *il faut être de son temps* – but it also means that online publications are continuously fighting for the reader's attention. Online attention is a constant battle. Apart from the traffic of a site, web analytics also measure how much time a given person will spend on this or that website. Five minutes is not bad at all. The economy of attention online is radically different than anything known in print. "Though we all spent hours each day scanning screens for information, what on the internet did we actually *read*?", [5] ask the editors of *Triple Canopy*, whose (much repeated) mantra is to "slow down the internet." Text has a built-in duration: we take a few milliseconds to recognize words; being image literate also means that even those seconds may seem like much. "Slowing down the internet" seems like one way in, both textually and visually: "Our thinking of images in relationship to economies of attention is no different than how we consider writing," says *Triple Canopy*'s Hannah Whitaker. "The photographs that we publish might require more attention and consideration than others online. We cater to a readership that accepts expending time and effort on a piece." The process of contextualizing online images, among the amazing diversity of the web, takes time. Demanding that the reader spend this time with the magazine is in fact quite refreshing and may push the viewer to, indeed, read online.

Another possible answer to the question of what content online do we actually read is built-in to mobile devices' interfaces. Ironically enough, even though mobile devices are supposedly designed to keep us company in transit (even considering the fact that Apple now advertises the iPad as a handheld device meant mainly for people who tend to sit on the couch most of the time, and don't want to walk over to their macbooks), the relatively new idea of apps actually introduces a new sense of undivided attention online. iOS, Apple's mobile operating system, does not really allow for simultaneous use of two apps. The result is that while on our computer we always have another tab open on the browser, another program open in the background, or another memo blinking on the calendar view, when we use the internet on our mobile devices, we focus on the app we are using. Reading the *New York Times* on its dedicated app doesn't allow for a quick change to look at the new email that just came in without leaving the newspaper app and switching to the email one – a decision much more conscious than that of switching tabs, for example. The iPad, iPhone, and other handheld devices also rid themselves of the cursor, so that their users are not really directed anywhere anymore. This is an interaction that designers are apparently much challenged by – a way of looking at a page that is closer to reading print. Where the cursor was a stand-in for the user's finger, the finger is now used again, and the eye follows a part of the body rather than an element embedded in the screen.

Now that such a screen-based platform exists, how to use it? "No one reads *Mousse* from cover to cover – and I'd imagine the iPad app is the same," says Cernuschi.

"When it comes to attention, I think it is also a derivative of the way in which information is presented graphically. We try to work with reduction – when the quantity of textual and visual content you can upload is limitless, it gets quite difficult – and we didn't want to be a Wikipedia kind of experience. We use one font across the range, keep the text simple, and try to focus on the images."

Cernuschi moves on to explain, "In a way, we're all children of the iPod." The act of using a touch screen is so pleasurable, such a radically different movement, scrolling with one's finger rather than flipping through paper, that it changes the user's interaction with the visual content. What the editors at *Mousse* claim was difficult in the development of the app is its boundless nature. In print, every addition might be translated to printing costs – so physical constraints bring about the necessity of making choices, and with it, an editorial line. Which led the editors to understand the iPad as a reading platform – "it's still two-dimensional," say Cernuschi – and so the app is not completely based on multimedia, even though it does include a number of videos, for example. But the shift from a printed copy of *Mousse* to its iPad app is not as sweeping as one may imagine.

The Location of the Online Image

When requesting images for a print publication, some guidelines are quite clear: the digital image needs to be 300dpi, it needs to be of a certain size, measured in inches and centimeters rather than pixels, and (at least usually) the rights for it need to be cleared. [6] Online publishing muddles all of these. While some of the publications contacted for this article attested that they have a photo editor or image editor (the leap to "image editor" in order to describe publishing in the online sphere is slowly being made. As

Whitaker noted, "It points to an opening up of the field to include the non-photographic image"), their role is more curatorial than that of a traditional editor. Are there any rules as to which images are published, the way they are retrieved, and their integration in the magazines? Surely, many images are harvested from a variety of online repository, Google Images being the obvious example. This nods to the flattening of the digital image in a complicated way. On screen, the different kinds of images – say, film stills, digital or analogue photography, digital renderings, and so forth – can be quite similar. While we are becoming increasingly visually literate, few are the people who truly interact with the distinction between the digital image and the physical print. No one is stunned anymore by the idea of a collector buying a photograph based on an image sent to him or her via email from a gallery. The printing process – moving from the screen to the physical object, that is – becomes a formality. In her introduction to *Triple Canopy*'s issue on photography, "Black Box," Whitaker points out the fact that a large number of the images found online (be they images uploaded to social networks, news-related ones, or commercial photographs) were shot digitally and uploaded to the internet, without, according to her, "so much as a passing consideration of printing them in a physical form." [7]

The Center for Curatorial Studies at Bard College recently introduced *Red Hook*, an online journal for curatorial studies. *Red Hook*'s relationship with images is one example that truly considers the magazine's online existence and presence. In the editorial for the first issue, its editor Tirdad Zolghadr states, "Although this journal will certainly attempt to do justice to opportunities for revisiting traditional hierarchies between image and text, it will be careful not to imply that language is diminishing in comparative importance, or that the online sphere can heal old wounds. On the contrary, the idea is to highlight and complicate an enduring hegemony in the hermeneutic food chain of online circulation." [8] One way to complicate those old wounds Zolghadr mentions – the text/image divide being a painful one – is the magazine's particular approach to images. Issue 1 is fully illustrated by one artist project: Katya Sander's *Hard Drive* [9], where all images accompanying the texts are automatically pulled from the web, based on each reader's hard drive as well as key words and themes in the articles. *Red Hook* does not have an image editor, but rather, it recruits artists to think through and further explore the magazine's relationship to images. Zolghadr explains,

"This was not meant to delegate image-editing responsibilities, at least not in a lazy and self-effacing way, but to avoid putting the cart before the horse. In a curatorial context, the specific mode of knowledge production I find the most productive is one that is developed and tested via an imbrication of theory and practice, saying and doing – preferably though not necessarily in tandem with artists. When Sander was invited to partake in the first issue, the instrumentalization of images in a publication context – and the lack of online signposts that traditionally steer this kind of process – was a cornerstone of the conversation."

The resulting project is refreshing – haven't seen an image repeated twice in the issue – and also confusing – the images accompanying the texts on my screen varied from milk bottles in a crate to demonstrators in Eastern Europe, and the link to the images' original contexts may be an interesting addition, but one that can be distracting, in that it sends the reader back to the wilderness of online image repositories, asking him or her to make sense of the images once those no longer have any relationship to the original text where they were encountered. It may be an interesting exercise in decoding images, but it's also a losing hand in the battle on online attention.

From Print to Screen and Back Again (from print to screen):

"When *Triple Canopy* was founded," its editors recall, "the content was bounded in a box and you 'flipped' through the pages as you would a print magazine. We hoped that this page metaphor would underline our relationship the kind of serious content more associated with printed media – to (as we've often stated) 'slow down the internet.' In the end, this format proved to be limiting and, ultimately, anathema to our mission to consider the internet's specific qualities as a form. We eventually redesigned the magazine and scrapped the page in favor of horizontally scrolling columns. In this new format, the relationships between image and text are more fluid. A given image is seen in the context of text that comes both before and after it and the bounds of the magazine are constrained by the size of the browser window and by the computer's screen size, or are in other words, set by the reader."

What this description exemplifies is the way in which the design of web-based art publications considers itself in face of print. The design of numerous online art publications considers the history and tradition of print in a myriad of nostalgic, more or less skeumorphic ways while bringing up old fears that reading habits are almost unchangeable. Even though *Triple Canopy* is quite unique in its horizontal scroll, it shares a similar attention to the print versus screen reading experience. One interesting element of which is the persisting presence of the table of contents in web-based publications: as part of the linking culture of the internet, the links to the other articles in the same issue are visible across the board. Another aspect of online culture that these publications have picked up on is tagging by subject and "for further reading" tabs, which try to anticipate the reader's interests according with the stated themes of a given article.

14

Where do images fall within these design questions? *Triple Canopy*'s editors attest that, "One issue that came up in the transition between the two formats [the flip box and the horizontal scroll] is that you lose the impact of a photograph when it slides onto the page rather than appearing in an instant. But, we do have a full screen function for those images that require more white space around them." Most other publications have a vertical design that introduces images as sidebars or directly aligned in the text, mainly without linking the images out or allowing for a full-screen viewing option. I would argue that this is another remnant of print culture in the digital sphere. Considering that the content of these online publications generally sways toward the theoretical more so than the glossy-print-magazine type, this brings forth a relationship with images where they are more illustrative and do not require a very specific – say, full-screen view – attention. *Mousse*'s Cernuschi says,

"We have a complicated relationship with images because we print in a newspaper format but we're a fine arts magazine. So we flirt with this idea of inaccurate reproduction in the first place. The priority with images is not exactly to 'get it,' – for that, I think paper printing is a very honest filter: it looks cool, but not really good. On the screen, images look much better. I would much prefer an image printed on appropriate paper than on a screen, but that's usually not the case. So for us it's very different, especially considering that we can reproduce media. You develop a so-called video still aesthetic on paper."

(and back again):

When considering the multiplicity of valid reasons why so many contemporary art publications choose to go online, it is quite astonishing to see how extensively they consider print as an option. [10] Take *e-flux journal*: it was launched by an organization that made its name and brand by being the first to give a very specific – and much called-for – online service. The journal, too, started in 2008 as a web-based initiative; but it soon introduced a series of readers in book form, published in collaboration with the Berlin-based publishing house Sternberg Press, and a print-on-demand system that allows readers and institutions to print out full issues followed. *e-flux journal*'s distribution system includes art institutions and bookstores around the world, who all download a PDF generated directly from the online articles, in what is a nod to ideas of open circulation and transmission of ideas on the internet, only in an offline, widely distributed but still independent, version.

A number of other web-based magazines seem inclined to follow *e-flux journal*'s direction. *Triple Canopy* published a first reader, *Invalid Format*, in the end of 2011. The cover of the book reads "Volume 1" – and indeed, the reader only covers issues 1 through 4, bringing up the amusing question of whether *Triple Canopy* will forever chase its own tail: Will the book-form readers catch up with the online journals? And *Red Hook* editor Zolghadr states that publishing a reader could be one direction for the magazine, but according to him "we're taking these things pedantically seriously, and are in no hurry to expand to other media just yet. The journal will first need to take its time to familiarize itself with its technical and institutional specificities."

So what does it mean to print out the internet? In the introduction to *Invalid Format*, the editors of *Triple Canopy* discuss their initial speculations as to the possible longevity of a web-based publication: "We had a sense of the inevitability of obsolescence – think of cassette tapes, LaserDiscs, Mosaic Netscape 0.9 – and of the need to safeguard our work being reduced to so many broken links and 404 errors." The idea of publishing books based on the online journal came up as a way of "artful archiving."

Downloading, so to say, the content of these publications from the online sphere to print can also introduce new problem of design. When taken offline, the images gain a new visual character: whereas on the screen, all images are in color but are indiscernible in context (especially when linked out of the specific journal – an image used in an online publication is totally different when viewed through Google Images) and in origin, in a printed form it is tied in with the text and the design in a way that relates to the history of publishing and to our expectations as readers in a wholly different way. Take, for example, Boris Groys's article, "The Weak Universalism," in *e-flux journal* [11]. The piece, where Groys considers avant-garde's nondistinction between artists and non-artists, is accompanied by a number of images, like a photograph of Kasimir Malevich teaching a class, a painting by Kandinsky, and a screenshot of Andy Warhol's Facebook page ("Sign up for Facebook to connect with Andy Warhol!"). The randomness of the screenshot may seem more intentional in print – in the print version of that issue, for example, it sits on the same spread as a still from *Empire* – and it loses interconnected nature that it may have with its online home (imagine reading that article on one browser tab while keeping Facebook open in another tab). And, unlike traditional print, where a screenshot or a video still may be of visibly lesser quality than a high-resolution photograph of a Kandinsky, the printed versions of online art publications tend to retain the flattened-out, non-hierarchical nature of the image as it was seen online. But whether images printed in poor quality, off the internet, become simply signifiers or rather, an "aesthetic of screenshots," remains with the reader.

To end at the beginning, let me bring up the question of the escalator one more time. Unlike an elevator or stairs, which can be featured in private homes or apartment buildings, an escalator is generally inherently public. It's not the exact middle ground between the stairs and the elevator because it picks up on certain elements of both while remaining a different variant of them as a mode of transport. Like the stairs, it considers only the human body (it will barely tolerate a baby carriage or luggage); and like the elevator, it has a built-in sense of pace. It seems pertinent here that the escalator is a trope of public space – train stations, airport, department stores, and so forth. What are the needs of the escalator riders? It allows them the possibility of cutting distances short while eliminating the sense of a group that an elevator may create.

The specificities of contemporary art publishing initiatives online may echo the escalator at times, while also embodying certain characteristics of the stairs and the elevator. We are only getting more image-savvy with time, which confuses and collides the relationship between text and images. The current decade is a very particular one in the history of publishing, as it will be full of moments that will be declared to be decisive for the "fate of the book." And maybe books are like taking the stairs – it may be old-fashioned, but still seems natural, and our brain-eye coordination is accustomed to it in a way similar to how quickly toddlers learn to crawl and walk up and down stairs. But the elevator? Standing in a slow-moving elevator seems more nerve wrecking than walking up the stairs. This is what reading an old e-book will be like one day.

The need for constant reinvention in digital publishing calls for a certain flexibility, and one that online art publications seem to be offering simply by the sheer fact of their constant consideration of what publishing online means. A hybrid model of print-to-screen-and-back-again might teach us much about our relationship with images, which will define and shape the history of art and the way it is taught and written about in coming years. This might just be the equivalent of the possibility to run up or down the escalator in the opposite direction than it is heading. It's possible, even if exhausting.

But sometimes, you just want to stand there on the escalator and see the ground distance itself from you while you take in the view.

First published on *Rhizome* on May 16, 2012. Available online at
http://rhizome.org/editorial/2012/may/16/screen-image-text/

ORIT GAT is a writer, editor, and translator based in New York. She is the senior editor
of *Modern Painters* magazine and a regular contributor to *Rhizome*.

Notes

[1] See http://moussemagazine.it.
[2] See http://canopycanopycanopy.com.
[3] See www.eastofborneo.org.
[4] Thomas Lawson, "The Journey West," on *East of Borneo*, October 10,
2010. Online at www.eastofborneo.org/articles/the-journey-west.
[5] Triple Canopy, "The Binder and the Server," *Art Journal*, vol. 70, n. 2: winter
2011, 40–57. Online at http://artjournal.collegeart.org/?p=2644.
[6] The "wild west" of online reproduction but intellectual property rights in
the internet environment is an incredibly complex subject that is currently
tackled by people in many fields in a constant attempt to define it for
themselves. The question of best practices for online reproduction and online
intellectual property rights is too large to consider seriously here and the
literature about it is slowly building.
[7] Whitaker's introduction deals with the space of photography in
contemporary society and how the elusive terminology of "images"
(converting all photographs, illustrative drawings, film stills, and so forth to
one all-encompassing class – which can mainly be characterized by the fact
that the people who view it do not often think about those images' origins) in
a way this article could never do. See her essay, "A Note on Black Box," in
Triple Canopy, issue 12.
[8] See Zolghadr's editorial, "Notes from the Editor," in *Red Hook*, issue 1.
Online at www.bard.edu/ccs/redhook/notes-from-the-editor/.
[9] For more informations on the project, see
www.bard.edu/ccs/redhook/hard-drive-an-experiment-in-intervisuality/.
[10] The idea of the possible obsolescence of online media and the fact that
technology seems to be developing at a pace much more rapid than the pace
of editorial decision is cheekily picked up by Zolghadr in his editorial:
"Curatorial education aside, a second moving target here, one that is at least

as mystifying, perhaps even more so, is the new field of online publishing. This is where you get an even clearer sense of the privilege and vertigo of inhabiting a historical threshold, leading to a constant suspicion that you're missing key conversations unfolding concurrently all around you, coupled with yet another nagging suspicion, that much of your eagerness and anxiety will be considered quaint only a few years from now."
[11] Boris Groys, "The Weak Universalism", in *e-flux journal*, Issue 15, April 2010. Online at www.e-flux.com/journal/the-weak-universalism/.

The Piracy Project

The Impermanent Book

21

Right: *No se lo digas a nadie* by Jaime Bayly; left: pirated copy with two extra chapters added by an anonymous writer. Bought in Lima Peru. The Piracy Collection

A few months ago, Jonathan Franzen, author of *The Corrections* and *Freedom*, was quoted by *The Telegraph* [1] from his Cartagena's Hay Festival presentation:

"Maybe nobody will care about printed books 50 years from now, but I do. When I read a book, I'm handling a specific object in a specific time and place. The fact that when I take the book off the shelf it still says the same thing – that's reassuring... and he goes on... Someone worked really hard to make the language just right, just the way they wanted it. They were so sure of it that they printed it in ink, on paper. A screen always feels like we could delete that, change that, move it around. So for a literature-crazed person like me, it's just not permanent enough."

His speech raised heated discussions in newspaper columns and on the internet. The focus was mainly on defending technology and e-books as a viable and improved evolution, and on how he was being retrograde. What was missing from the discourse was the fact that technology has also violently altered printed books in a way from which there is no return. We are so disconnected from the means of production that nobody seems to be aware that books are produced very differently then they were 100 years ago. Digital files are exchanged between writers, publishers and printers all over the world.

In the context of the Piracy Project, which we initiated in London in 2010, we discovered cases, which not only took control over the object, but over the content. Inspired by Daniel Alarcon's article in *Granta* magazine, "Life Among Pirates" [2], we traveled to Peru and discovered, for instance, a pirated version of Jaime Bayly's novel *No se lo digas a nadie* with two extra chapters added. This physical object may look obviously pirated to a trained eye but could easily pass as the original if you were not looking for differences. The extra chapters are good, good enough to pass undetected by readers.

These books are sold in small markets, bookshops or by street vendors at traffic crossings. We had to buy several books and to compare page by page until we found a book with extra content. Asking the vendors for help didn't work. They were quite offended with the insinuation that they carried modified books. Buyers don't want to read a book by an anonymous author when they are buying Mario Vargas Llosa.

Friends in Peru seemed extremely surprised to see an altered book. The same type of trust that Franzen had applied to printed books was broken. What have they been reading? According to popular literary theory, when reading a book we become joint authors by virtue of subjectively interpreting and shifting the context through our own personal sets of experience. In this sense, it might be very difficult to realize, in discussion with others, whether or not the book you just read has been altered. And then what happens when that seed of distrust is planted in your head?

A similar experience was reported by a friend when she grabbed one of the copies of Franzen's novel *Freedom* that was accidentally printed from an earlier draft and distributed in London for a few weeks before being re-called, destroyed and replaced by the "correct" version. Knowing that there were mistakes in the text, or passages that had been added made her read the text in a very suspicious manner. There were quite a few passages where she was completely sure she had spotted one of the "wrong" bits. "I'll never know if I was right in my suspicions." she said "Comparing the two versions seemed like too much work. Anyway, I quite like the idea of having read the text in this undefined space."

The modified books in Peru are a direct result of technological changes. Older pirated books looked more like photocopies. Re-typing a whole novel is a lot of work and inserting new content would be demanding. Currently, pirated books are produced using original text files stolen from the publishers or a pdf in transit to the printers.

A respectable percentage of all the books in the world are currently printed in the Guangzhou province in China. The distance between publishers and printers embedded in a local culture, which has a different understanding of copying and its moral implications has created an interesting phenomenon. China is not only inundated with pirated versions of western books (which many suspect may be simply cases of printers printing extra copies of the originals) but it also has generated an interesting number of "curators," who select material from all these different publications and collate new volumes – a bizarre reflection of internet content curators.

The piracy of architecture books is very common in China and vendors regularly visit architectural practices carrying a specially tailored selection. It's a mixture of our contemporary curatorial culture and Chris Anderson's Long Tail theory. The Architectural Association in London, for example, seems to be quite influential. It was the only university press we encountered on our visits that deemed worth the extra expense of translation. Chinese architects proved not to be that popular, but Rem Koolhaas is a best seller. It is interesting to note how the selection of books for sale made by the pirate sellers and the cross-contamination of taste and interest they carry from one office to the other could be one of the defining elements of how urban China is going to look in the next twenty years. But some of these copies are not simple mechanical translations. We found a copy of a pirated *Mark* magazine which seemed condensed from six other *Mark* issues and edited down into this one edition. We bought it fascinated with the idea that somebody had gone through the issues selecting what they considered important. But after comparing it with the originals we realized that the process wasn't that obvious. It was the whole content of just one issue – only a full-page photograph showing a female Chinese architect was removed – with added pages from an unidentified Italian magazine, which was left in Italian.

We see similar tendencies in contemporary publishing. For instance, AND Public, another AND Publishing project exploring the potential of print-on-demand (POD). It is a platform for artists, writers and curators to use the possibility of printing books in very small numbers as they get distributed. The project gives users a distribution structure that tries to solve the biggest question in self-publishing: I made my book now how do I find its public?

But it also raises questions of how books exist as permanent objects. In traditional publishing one version of a book is printed. Any new edition may bring corrections or modifications, but each is clearly attributed. With print-on-demand, the author has the option to keep changing their artwork and re-printing the book. "Editions" or versions of the book are not necessarily identified.

Zadie Smith spoke at the New York Public Library in 2011 about her observations at literary festivals. She saw writers sitting behind curtains at literary festivals, armed with red pens, correcting their own two year old books just before their readings. This was a unique chance to re-address the text and to make real the book they wished they had written. With AND Public, as with many other POD platforms, to re-write is a concrete and constant possibility. There won't be a guarantee that the POD book you bought is identical with the next buyer's book. In fact, many artists use this mutable production process as an intrinsic part of their work and keep changing their texts to test the conceptual boundaries of the book.

In the beginning of recorded history, books used to be copied by hand and constantly modified through these interpretations. It is the technological advances of the analog printing press that construct our contemporary idea of books as fixed objects, where immutability is a key factor that allows for mass and consistent reproduction. But now, with digital printing technologies, mass production and mutability live hand in hand. The values and attributes that define books are much more malleable than we wish to face and, once again, we must be diligent of where knowledge is being generated. It is undeniable that books are an incredible technology that will most likely never be abandoned, but that doesn't mean they will remain the same. They have never remained the same.

First published on *Rhizome* on April 19, 2012. Available online at
http://rhizome.org/editorial/2012/apr/19/impermanent-book/

THE PIRACY PROJECT is an international publishing and exhibition project exploring
the philosophical, legal and practical implications of book piracy and creative modes of
reproduction. Through an international call for contributions, The Piracy Project has
gathered a collection of more than one hundred modified, appropriated and copied
books from artists across the world. The collection, which is catalogued online, is the
starting point for talks and workgroups around the concept of originality, the notion of
authorship and politics of copyright.
The Piracy Project is a collaboration between AND Publishing and Andrea Francke.
AND (www.andpublishing.org) is a platform exploring new digital technologies to
publish conceptual artists' books run by Lynn Harris and Eva Weinmayr. Digital print-
on-demand is defined as a tool to directly interact with an audience. Due to short print
runs and low productions costs, AND can sustain an adventurous and inquiring
creative practice without having to conform to the mass market.

Notes

[1] Cf. Anita Singh, "Jonathan Franzen: e-books are damaging society", in
The Telegraph, January 29, 2012.
[2] Daniel Alarcón, "Life Among the Pirates", in Granta, Issue 109: Work,
Winter 2009. Online at www.granta.com/Archive/Granta-109-Work/Life-
Among-the-Pirates/.

28

Rahel Aima

The Web That Can't Wait

29

Silvio Lorusso, Sebastian Schmieg, *56 Broken Kindle Screens*, 2012. Image courtesy the artists

One of my earliest memories is getting hit in the face by a book. I was two; we had just moved to Dubai, and were staying with another family for the first few weeks. While we were playing, their younger son threw his book at me. It cut open the thin skin below my right eye, just above the line now demarcated by insomnia's purplish bruisings. I remember only fragmented flashes. The green Small World Library hardback with Goofy on its cover, the tears, and the blood – so much blood that the book retained a rusty stain on the spine.

The scar has since stretched and faded to a gathered curve, barely discernible to the touch and perceptible only if you know where to look. As I grew, I accrued many other scars, each with its own story, but this one remained special: my own facial bookmark.

Like a tribal mark or that left arm vaccine scar that quietly signifies which global sphere you're from, I had been struck by the weight of a book.

And read I did, as if to fill up this hole that the book had gouged in my face – compulsively and voraciously, and at every snatched moment I could. Yet Dubai's public library system was anaemic at best, and its bookstores, with their politely aligned new titles, antiseptic. Summer visits to India became all the more rarified as a result. Here, finally, pavements were hedged with booksellers, and inside, up rickety staircases and under the eye of equally rickety old men, were shelves heaving with books. These bookstores smelled like the ones I had read about: all heady with the intoxicating lignin of tomes gone to seed, mixed in with that slightly musty dampness unique to monsoon season.

Even in this bibliophilic paradise, however, lurked a sense of spoilage, insistently asserting itself like the background static of an AC. No matter how greedily I read and reread, I could never hope to possibly open – let alone own – even a fraction of the books I saw. And that's to say nothing of all the books I had never even heard of, but was still painfully aware were out there.

Later on, college would highlight in relief just how much I hadn't read. Each semester I took far more courses than I could legitimately handle, and reading became consumptive instead of submersive. It became good enough to quickly read each text just once; a slower savoring could come later. On visits home, I would fill my suitcase with that semester's texts in hopes of rereading them – properly, this time – but they always remained in accusative stacks on the floor, neglected in favor of my childhood favorites. As much as I wanted to build a library and surround myself with books, NYC storage concerns colluded with a sense of self-exhorted acceleration to shift my primary reading format from books, to PDFs, to Twitter and tabbed browsing.

Here, again, was that same urgency transposed from page to screen. Do you know the feeling? That sharp, almost adrenal jolt when you open just one more tab and all the favicons disappear to give you a segmented line of characters? You can't increase your screen resolution much more, but keep the pages open, just on the off chance that you might actually read them. Perhaps you quickly scan in order to close a tab, yet find yourself clicking on "History" just moments later, just in case you missed something. Perhaps you feel guilty about not giving each piece the undivided attention you once lavished upon your books, but often, just knowing the dust jacket-like gist seems to be enough. You consider developing an Instapaper habit, but don't trust that you will ever train yourself to go back, sit down, and read them at leisure. Because should you manage the impossible, and find time to actually read them after the fact, won't it be too late? Won't the conversation have moved on?

This kind of pearl clutching over time poverty and the whirling hyperkineticism of the Web is nothing new. A few decades into the Internet, the browser has become cemented as the new battleground. At face, debates about the experience of reading online rest on a collective nostalgia for the book as an aesthetic object. What's really at stake is the practice of reading itself: when, where, and on whose platform.

Relevant here is what Jack Cheng has conceptualized as the 'Slow Web Movement,' using the metaphor of slow and fast foods [1]. In the Fast Web ("a cruel wonderland of shiny shiny things") our timelines, dashboards, inboxes, and RSS readers are overflowing with dubiously recycled styrofoam. Against this real-time heartburn – overcalorific and cholesterol laden – he suggests we instead privilege timeliness. That we forgo the whizzy randomness of the Fast Web in favor of a compartmentalized sense of rhythm, consuming media only when we have the time to give them our full attention. Instapaper becomes reframed as 'turn based reading,' while email becomes similarly gamified as 'turn based communication.' "What next?" becomes "when next?" Coupled with portion control, specialist apps, and productivity systems, the Slow Web ethos promises a healthier, happier, more self-satisfied life. Or to refashion Michael Pollan's food rules: Read online. Not too much. Mostly *#longform*.

My biggest beef with the Slow Web Movement, however? It hinges on self control and delayed gratification, and moderation was never my strong suit. I've never been able to maintain a Google Reader or productively use any kind of RSS service; ludicrous as it may sound, I read everything at source. No matter how much I organize and breadcrumb subscriptions, I can't shake the feeling that I'm missing out. Rather than limit myself to the curated CSA inboxed newsletters, I want to devour it all; what was once an ambient AC hum is now more akin to roaring static. It's a tower of Babel out there in the world wide web, and I love that about it.

Robin Sloan's *Fish App* [2] for iOS takes another approach to recreating an immersive reading experience. Its design is arresting – pastelised and in full screen, you are straitjacketed into focusing on just one quiet sentence or phrase at a time. To move through the essay, you tap the screen; there is no back button. Sloan juxtaposes the qualitative differences between liking or favoriting, and loving, noting that when we love something on the internet, we "pluck them out of the flood and put them on shelves and playlists and home screens." We put them in places where we can see, and easily return to them. Watching something twice becomes a radical act; reading something twice is one of love. Yes, you can download things to read later, but the ultimate problem with the Internet, in his estimation, is that it has no album view. Put another way, the problem with the Internet is that it is difficult to build a library.

How then do you return to things on the Internet? And what does it mean to amass a digital library, and not an archive? Is it about the visual metaphor, about displaying your links and files on an iOS-like interface? The ability to browse your collection, to see it in shelves and stacks and file folders instead of just calling it up via a search?

With finite disk space, however, comes the familiar old storage anxieties – even the *Fish App*, in its very form, dredges up the spectre of home screen clutter. Despite your best attempts at a taxonomy of spareness, hard drives fill up quickly with PDFs and MP3s. You devise new rules to spring clean your digital hoard: if you haven't watched or listened to this file in a year, into the bin it goes. Ikea unfortunately doesn't make storage solutions for files; unlike physical books, they are all too easy to delete.

So the tabs stay open. They haunt you, and perhaps guilt you with baleful, anthropomorphized glares. In a way, they are a discursive equivalent of the decidedly frenzied urban condition, 'fomo,' [3] or 'fear of missing out.' On events, on parties, on shows, on things that you should have already read and be conversant about. So you get on the train; so you open a new tab. It's much the same with books – piled up on tables, Jengaed on the floor, waiting. As if owning and beginning the book is tantamount to having read it; as if by surrounding yourself, you might magically learn by pure osmosis.

And now I'm thinking of these gorgeous, searing lines from Nicholas Rombes' "Julia Kristeva's Face," [4] which have remained screenburned into my head since I first read them:

The Kristeva book was like a hot coal. It burned through desks and tables and the seats of chairs. It singed the carpeting. It glowed at night in a regurgitated blood orange. It misplaced itself. It flipped itself over in the dark like a fish. I had to put a brick on it to keep it still.

That pneumatic urgency, where a book bristles, and demands, and makes its presence felt? You have to actually first begin reading, and get stuck in. Except – unlike tabs, unlike files, unlike the now-you-see-it-now-it's-404 current underwriting the internet, books won't leave you, and instead stay, patiently stacked until they are read. But what if this wasn't the case? What if the books on your shelves began to wipe themselves with time, a reader's nightmare akin to the writer's productivity app, *Write or Die* [5] on kamikaze mode? Argentinian indie publishers Eterna Cadencia have created just that, with *The Book That Can't Wait*, an anthology of new authors. The book is printed with a special ink that begins to fade as soon as it is opened and exposed to sun and air, with the words disappearing completely within two months.

My instant reaction is positive. Their explanatory video [6] is rich, slickly produced, and tugs at all the right bibliophilic heartstrings. As they explain, "There's a lot of literature out there that doesn't deserve to wait on the shelf. And ours won't wait at all." Like the talking avatars dissecting experiences of online reading, Eterna Cadencia are trying their best to renegotiate the way we read online – when, where, and using whose hardware. Instead of slowing down reading to the measured rhythms of the codex, however, *The Book That Can't Wait* speeds it up to the frenetic tempo of tabbed browsing. And in a landscape already saturated with lazy skeuomorphism, it seems hard to argue against. Why slavishly make the screen look more like a page when you can make the page feel more like a screen?

Aesthetics aside, it's important to interrogate what this kind of marketing strategy actually means. Who benefits? The publisher, certainly, and perhaps the authors, if only for the publicity. The reader, however, loses a lot: the ability to keep a beloved, dog eared book around for years, to dip in and out of it at will, and to lend, gift, or resell their copy; to build a library. As for booksellers, already beleaguered in the best of economies? An entire ecosystem of second-hand bookstores, both brick-and-mortar and online, will crumble, as will prison literacy-type programs, that sustain themselves upon donated materials.

The disappearing ink technology in itself opens up some broader questions. Used for newspapers, flyers, office printouts and other limited-use ephemeral literature, it could revolutionize paper use and recycling – albeit with the risk of creating a new hierarchy of printed matter. More chillingly, it can be seen as an analogue application of DRM to the printed page, following in the footsteps of the e-book. Recall Amazon's deliciously Orwellian blunder in which it remotely deleted copies of *Animal Farm* and *1984* from Kindles over copyright claims. [7] In the process, it alienated customers who were shocked that something they had purchased was not theirs to keep. In some cases, people even lost their annotations and notes in the margin – original, sometimes scholarly work – which raised further questions of ownership and impermanence.

Returning to that early recollection of getting cut open by the crushing physicality of a book, I called my mother. To ask about the incident, about the gushing blood, and did I have to get stitches? She sounds surprised I remember it, and tells me it was not much more than a little nick. Not much blood, no fuss, and certainly no surgery. That was memory, writ in an equally precarious kind of disappearing ink. For it to be remotely debunked and wiped clean – reformatting my early childhood, in a way – so neatly is unsettling.

When we enthuse about print books, we talk about them like they'll be around forever. Such is not the case; like memories and scars, they fade and warp over time. Consider the spectrum from mass-market paperbacks that very quickly become unbound and jaundiced with age, through to more expensive texts that might be printed on acid-free paper. Rarer texts get a panoply of preservation treatments from binding and display cases through to environmental controls that limit exposure to heat and light. In their attempt to rejuvenate print, Eterna Cadencia just might be sounding the death knell, in insisting that we treat each book with the white-gloved, sacralized care we accord to museum and archival pieces.

I'm imagining, too, what future bookstores might look like if more publishers adopt the technology. Perhaps they will come to more closely resemble hypermarket cold rooms, with sterilized, vac-packed books. Next to the register, a wall of single-or-multiple use shellacs, that reveal the invisible ink, and grant you a painted on-access to your words for a limited time. A new cottage industry of dry cleaners that chemically treat and process your books to make them legible for a time. And small, microbial clusters of stealth cells, in several nowheres, gather together each week to figure out how to hack the page.

First published on *Rhizome* on August 24, 2012. Available online at
http://rhizome.org/editorial/2012/aug/24/slow/

RAHEL AIMA is co-editor at http://THESTATE.ae. Currently based between dxb-bk.

Notes

[1] Cf. Jack Cheng, "The Slow Web", June 2012, online at
http://blog.jackcheng.com/post/25160553986/the-slow-web. More info at
http://theslowweb.com/.
[2] Available online at www.robinsloan.com/fish/.
[3] Cf. Caterina Fake, "FOMO and Social Media", in *Caterina.net*, March 15,
2011. Online at http://caterina.net/2011/03/15/fomo-and-social-media/.
[4] Nicholas Rombes, "Julia Kristeva's Face", in *The Rumpus*, June 14, 2011,
online at http://therumpus.net/2011/06/julia-kristevas-face/.
[5] "Write or Die is a new kind of writing productivity application that forces
you to write by providing consequences for distraction and procrastination."
Cf. http://writeordie.com/.
[6] Available on YouTube at http://youtu.be/gHl8lqCqza8.
[7] Cf. Brad Stone, "Amazon Erases Orwell Books From Kindle", in *The New
York Times,* July 17, 2009. Online at www.nytimes.com/2009/07/18/
technology/companies/18amazon.html.

Angela Genusa

A Book Is Technology: An Interview with Tan Lin

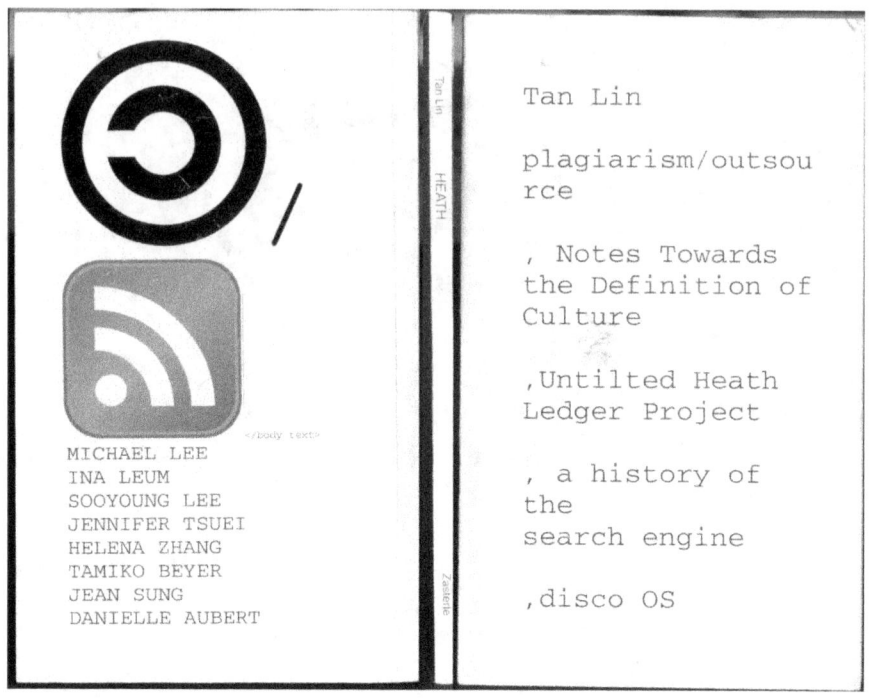

Tan Lin, *HEATH (plagiarism/outsource).* **Cover wrap, courtesy aphasic-letters.com.**

Over the past 15 years, poet, novelist, and filmmaker Tan Lin has been at work creating an "ambient" mode of literature that engages a set of practices including sampling, communal production, and social networks, addressing issues such as relaxed copyright, boredom, plagiarism, and the commodification of attention.

He has written 10 books, most recently "Seven Controlled Vocabularies and Obituary 2004. The Joy of Cooking" (2010); "Insomnia and the Aunt" (2011); and "Heath Course Pak" (2011). His video work has screened at the Yale Art Museum, Artists Space, the Drawing Center, and the Ontological Hysterical Theatre. He is currently finishing work on a novel, "OUR FEELINGS WERE MADE BY HAND". He teaches creative writing at New Jersey City University.

> We talked by Skype, G-chat, email, phone, and used Google
> Drive in real-time to talk about the many different uses of
> technology in his work and what its implications are for the future
> of literature.

**AG. In your books, especially *HEATH (plagiarism/
outsource)* and *Seven Controlled Vocabularies and
Obituary 2004. The Joy of Cooking* (from now on, *7CV*), you
introduced people to a new idea of what a book of
literature can be. For these books, in their various versions
and associated events, you incorporated everything from
email to Twitter, programming languages to RSS feeds,
Google Translate to Post-it notes. What led you to use so
many different forms of technology in the creation and
publication of a book? How would you define a book?**

TL. People forget that a book or codex is a technology. My
interest with *HEATH* and *7CV* was to treat the book as a distinct
medial platform through which a lot of ancillary information
passes, much like a broadcast medium like TV or a narrow-cast
medium like Twitter or Tumblr. Reading is information control,
just as a metadata tag is a bibliographic control. So I wanted to
highlight the book's medial and time-based underpinnings.

**AG. How would you prepare someone who has never read
a Tan Lin book to read one of your books?**

TL. It's a little hard to say. I think a book is something
consumed slowly over many years – it's a little like watching a
plant reproduce. What are *HEATH* and *7CV*? I'm not sure, but
maybe a delayed reading experience that involves Course Paks,
marketing departments of publishing houses, seminars at the
University of Pennsylvania, RSS feeds, and Post-it notes. And, of
course, other books – with *7CV, The Joy of Cooking* – and with
plagiarism/ outsource, blogs that chronicled Heath Ledger's death.
Why insert *The Joy of Cooking* into the title of *7CV*? Because it
was the cookbook my family used to become American and

because I thought the title would increase Google hits. I consider Google a mode of (loose) autobiography. A book in Google Books, like someone's search history, isn't really a book; it's data connected to other data, and it's searchable. Reading, like autobiography, is a subset of a search function.

AG. Why did you print Post-it notes in *HEATH*?

TL. After the Zasterle edition of *HEATH* came out, I was often asked to read from it, but it's long and I had difficulty controlling and seeing what I should be reading, or even seeing what's important, so I stuck Post-it notes to cover up parts of the text and in that way made a more streamlined and visible (at least to me!) version. It's like a paper map to me, inserted in a digital production. When the book was republished by Counterpath, we photographically reproduced the pages covered with Post-it notes. In the new edition, the Post-it notes look like you can run your fingers over them, but they're just photographs (of a book) after it gave up some textual matter. Books change over time and they're blind; they give up information as readily as they gain it. What is a book today? I have no idea.

AG. In an interview with Katherine Elaine Sanders for *BOMB*, you stated that "Reading is a kind of integrated software." [1] Could you elaborate on this?

TL. Integrated software is a genre of software that combines word processing, database management, spreadsheet applications, and communications platforms. This genre has been superseded by various full-function office suites, but I was interested in reading modeled in that way, i.e., different kinds of reading, each with specific functions. I mean, you read Harlequin romances differently than recipes, and you read Lotus 1-2-3 spreadsheets differently than you read Excel, and you read experimental Japanese novels differently than you read text messages, and in terms of documents processed by software, you have distinctions between, say, end-user manuals, bills of sales, Unified Modeling Language models, and legal contracts. These are genres of reading, and they're housed or processed in the same generic platform that I call "reading." So reading is an application that processes or assembles varied kinds of material. I was interested in creating works of literature that could be read like recipes or spreadsheets or PowerPoint presentations.

AG. What does the process of software authoring entail and why does it interest you?

TL. I think it's a way to talk about new modalities of reading. In software engineering, the authoring is sometimes implemented with what are called frames, where kinds of (reading or processing) functionality are packed into frames, and where a frame is "a generic component in a hierarchy of nested subassemblies" [2]. You'll have word processing frames and graphics frames, etc., and these individual frames can be linked in a unified programming system. This enables you to embed graphics and spreadsheet functions into a text document, or you can have shared graphical contexts, where material pops up in multiple frames at the same time – this, I think, is what is happening in *7CV* with its graphical elements, text elements, processing text instructions in the form of prefaces (so-called "source" material) and meta data tags. I also inserted other languages: Chinese and machine codes. *7CV* has various things in it that look like captions or interfaces or even bits of source code, and I was interested in the difference between a caption and bit of machine code in a book. If you look at the handwritten Chinese text in *7CV* (it was written by my mother) you'll notice that it was put in upside down by the typesetter! This is not true of the machine-generated Chinese, provided by Google Translate. But at any rate you have a complex ecosystem of different languages in single publishing/reading platform.

I assembled both PowerPoint works similarly. Bibliographic Sound Track was compiled from SMS, IM chats, video game walk-throughs, Tweets, Tumblr entries, PowerPoint bullet points, photographic slides, the overhead transparency, the text box, the couplet, the book page, the fading film titling sequence, etc. PowerPoint is a multimedia ecosystem that encompasses a wide variety of reading practices, and where each slide or page is a frame: modular, linked to other frames, and encompassing various platform specific reading or communications functions. So here was a generic poem, where a poem is the most varied collection of different material that could be read continuously in a time-based manner with a definite run time. Reading can be looped. That, I think, is the definition of a poem today!

AG. What are the differences between your PowerPoint works [3] and your print books?

TL. The most obvious difference is that when you read a book or codex, the only thing moving is your eye; with the PowerPoint works, both text and eye are moving. In this sense, PowerPoint makes reading autonomous and it sets it in motion, literally: Individual slides are animated, slide transitions are animated, and the piece overall is software that is processing information. That's why we turned out the lights during the screening and projected large: No one expects to go to the cinema and read a book on the screen, one word at a time, but that's kind of what I wanted to do. The most beautiful thing is a book that could read itself! So reading is a kind of integrated software or the frame technology that manufactures software, and a book is the software application that is manufactured.

But I think there are a lot of similarities between digital and print-based reading experiences. The PowerPoint pieces, like my books, all bracket reading in a larger perceptual (and social) field that includes smells and sounds, i.e., they situate reading in a larger geography or reading environment. People tend to forget that reading is a kind of all-over experience, and it takes place in a particular room or in a particular moment of childhood. So the idea was to not confine reading to a particular object (book) or platform (PowerPoint) but allow it to expand outwards into the social space around it. I was more interested in what might be called the general mood of reading: the overall atmosphere or medium in which we experience our daily thoughts and perform actions— what Heidegger termed Stimmung and the psychologist Daniel Stern calls affective or amodal attunements. *Bibliographic Sound Track* (2012) is a mood-based system, but so is *HEATH*. And these mood-based systems, which are common to Zen meditative states, are bottom-up, non-directed, allotropic modes of general receptiveness rather than top-down, attention-based focus on specific objects or things. A book, at bottom, is a very general and very generic thing (that we happen to be reading).

AG. But a Zen meditative state isn't reading is it?

TL. My print-based and web-based works both tend to operate with the minimum amount of material necessary needed to constitute what we call reading. I'm interested in the forms of non-reading and boredom, which surrounds all reading and aesthetic experience as its customary default. I mean I like it when works are boring. When I go to see a Cage performance or a Merce Cunningham dance, I am bored half the time. There's nothing wrong with that. *7CV* is about skimming material, appropriating other titles (like *The Joy of Cooking*) and indexes, and extending the book by enlisting 30+ grad students at The University of Pennsylvania to spin off what publishers would call ancillary titles. Can *7CV* be made more interesting by individual readers? Absolutely. This is common in academia, a profession defined by writing books about other books, i.e., generating secondary source material. But there's no reason secondary source material cannot be more interesting than original source material. Do you have to read *7CV* to have read it? Not at all. Moreover, there are many ways to not read a book: you can leaf through it, read reviews or synopses of it, or just lie and say you read it when you didn't. I was at Columbia where I got a Ph.D. in literature, and there were about 250 books on my orals reading lists – books I had to be able to talk about – but I probably only read a third of them. In fact, though, I had read all of them, just in different ways.

AG. *Bibliographic Sound Track* carried a perfume track and a live Twitter feed when it was projected at Artists Space, and *The Ph.D Sound* (2012) carried a live DJ set. Why did you present these pieces as you did?

TL. So that the reading was like a book only to the extent that the book is regarded as a porous, unstable, and provisional platform for the dissemination of information. We tend to think of books as interiorized devices, linked to solitude and self-enclosed spaces; and they deliver something, like meaning, up to the reader. But I'm not so interested in knowledge in that teleological sense; I'm more interested in the dissipation of knowledge, unfocused attention, and generic receptiveness. It would be nice if a book could reduce the amount of knowledge in the air. I'm equally interested in the public and communal architecture of reading practices as they intersect with individuals and park benches, the subway and the seminar room. Why can't a book be more like a perfume? Or a door? Or the year after we graduated from college? A perfume is a communications medium just as literature is. Moods, furniture, restaurants, and books are communications mediums. What is it that Warhol said? "I think the right hormones can make Chanel No. 5 smell very butch."

AG. So how is the experience of reading your works different from a more conventional novel or a Hollywood movie?

TL. Usually you go to a movie or read a book to experience an emotion: Hollywood and even independent cinema is excruciatingly good at eliciting (i.e., manipulating) feelings in the audience – that's why most people read novels and go to movies, and directors like Lars von Trier and Michael Haneke play with this by artificially manipulating an audience's emotions via specific cinematic genres. Michel Houellebecq does something similar with literature, but less effectively to my mind. Think about the tragedy of *Dancer in the Dark* presented as a Broadway musical! But I think that reading that ends in an emotion is lame; I like it more when literature generates not a distinct emotion or feeling but a more generalized overall mood, and I like this more because I think it's more reflective of the way we actually spend most of our lives. Psychologists have identified something like 6 major emotions, but the thing is we don't feel them very often, which is a good thing because most of them are quite unpleasant: disgust, fear, anger, etc.

AG. You've stated that some of *7CV* (and *plagiarism/ outsource – HEATH*) were "self-plagiarized," and obviously the title *The Joy of Cooking* was appropriated. What role does plagiarism and appropriation play in your work?

TL. Plagiarism is less meaningful as an economic concept today than it was 15 years ago, which is why, from a legal standpoint, at least if you follow Posner, it is connected to notions of detrimental reliance. When plagiarizing something adds to a work's value, or increases the number of page hits, which is common when you take something in the poetry world and redistribute it, then notions of plagiarism don't seem avantgarde at all. Take a look at publishing ventures that use Tumblr as a platform, such as *Troll Thread* [4], *sisteract* [5], and *Gauss PDF* [6]. Nor should *7CV* or *HEATH* be construed as avantgarde or difficult in that limited sense. With the migration to cloud-based computing and paywalls and unsearchable gardens, this is changing. Pretty soon, content will be tethered much more tightly, yoked to proprietary systems themselves like Facebook, and ideas of plagiarism as a strong concept will no doubt surface again. Both *7CV* and *HEATH* were about how information, like news or advertising or a meme, is meant to be circulated as much as possible. This is true of communications mediums generally but it used to be that literature was opposed to such ideas of free or unpaid circulation. So the first edition of *7CV* can still be downloaded free on Lulu.com or purchased as a perfect-bound book (it lacks a "real" cover) for less than the cost of the Wesleyan University Press edition. Suzanna Tamminen, the director of WUP, has not had any problem with this or at least she hasn't written me about it.

AG. How have your books been received?

TL. In the case of *HEATH*, it got bootlegged as soon as it went out of print after a few months. And you have to understand the economy of experimental poetry titles. *HEATH* was published in an edition of 300 by a small house in the Canary Islands. And there are various versions of *7CV*, many out of my control and put up on Lulu now by other authors. It's possible that they are more interesting together than apart, which is to say they are more interesting as communications mediums or blips in a publishing and distribution system than as literary mediums. *HEATH* has a copyleft agreement, which is a specific kind of licensing agreement, attached to it. A publishing house in Vienna, Westphalie Verlag, bootlegged the book last year, reprinting the volume and selling it without my knowledge. I think it got presented at the Berlin Art Book Fair this year but I'm not sure. In this case, the publisher did not have the image files for the web sites that I initially sampled – Blimpies and Jackie Chan Green Iced Tea – so when he re-sampled the corporate web sites, he got different images. So here, web-based photos lifted from corporate web sites functioned as a new (pictorial) date stamps for the edition, thereby extending the edition into a new time frame, where the book has a kind of time-keeping device or stopwatch built into it. I wish I had thought of this, but I didn't.

AG. How has Internet culture affected your work? How has it affected literature in general?

TL. Most of my recent work overlaps the development of what is called Web 2.0, although the PowerPoint works might encompass Web 3.0 – where the web appears to do one's thinking (or writing/ reading) for one. The movement of software to participatory, web-based platforms, along with the growth of user-generated content, informs both *7CV* and *HEATH*. Both these books are marked by real-time updating of materials, customization of existing content, an increasing interpenetration between digital formats and the physical artifact known as the book, most notably via metadata standards and folksonomies. In this sense, the model for reading, like book making, is changing. As I mentioned, literary studies represses its medial component – which is why literary studies is distinct from media studies at most universities. And literature generally tends to repress its time-based elements. So when you read Andrew Marvell's "To His Coy Mistress," [7] a poem that is all about time, most people don't care that they read line 2 at 3:36 and line 17 at 4:15 – but I think that's an altogether more interesting way to read literature. I like a novel with a stopwatch in it; but even more, I like a novel that is a stopwatch.

For me, I think of reading as data management rather than passive absorption on a couch, though these dichotomies are ultimately false. Reading is and probably always will be a bit of both. At any rate, ideas about information processing are altering the contours of printed and digital works. Suddenly the book is just one element in a larger system of textual controls, distribution models, and controlled vocabulary systems. This is certainly true of the two PowerPoint works. I mean, what are they? Are they poems or are they more like Twitter feeds? They don't seem like PowerPoint presentations because they're weak didactically and they don't make a point. They are inflected by communications devices, but they do have a rhythm, which poems tend to have! And likewise with Twitter. Is it a broadcast medium using a pull system much like an RSS feed? Or is it more of a storage device, like a scroll or a poem? The idea of a network as a platform for collaborative work (rather than software housed on an individual's desktop) might be applied to a book, no longer regarded as discrete, stand-alone object but as something that gets updated on a periodic basis in a social network. But this may not be that new an idea. After all, David Hume praised the printing press because it made it possible to issue countless emendations, revisions, and new editions.

AG. Can you state briefly what you see as the future of the book?

TL. Let's return for a moment to the bootleg by Westphalie Verlag in Vienna. Did the publisher David Jourdan in this case create what, under U.S. copyright law, would be termed "strong" copyleft where the derivative work is "based on the program" and has a "clear will to extend it to "dynamic linkage"? At this point, we are talking about software development licensing, shared libraries, primary access to source code, site linkages, share and share alike provisions, and software pools. My question is: Can a book be made to look like the authoring of such software, caught in a complicated licensing and development system? I think so! Maybe that's the future of the book: to look like a licensing agreement regarding the future dissemination of its own information.

First published on *Rhizome* on October 24, 2012. Available online at
http://rhizome.org/editorial/2012/oct/24/interview-tan-lin/.

ANGELA GENUSA is a writer, poet, and artist who lives in the US.

Notes

[1] Katherine Elaine Sanders, "Tan Lin", in *Bomb*, March 2010. Online at
http://bombsite.com/issues/999/articles/3467.
[2] Cf. "Frame technology (software engineering)", in *Wikipedia*, online at
http://en.wikipedia.org/wiki/Frame_technology_(software_engineering).
[3] Tan Lin's PowerPoint works are available online at
http://writing.upenn.edu/pennsound/x/Lin.php.
[4] Troll Thread, http://trollthread.tumblr.com/.
[5] Sisteract, http://sisteract.tumblr.com/.
[6] Gauss PDF, http://www.gauss-pdf.com/.
[7] "To His Coy Mistress is a metaphysical poem written by the English author
and politician Andrew Marvell (1621–1678) either during or just before the
Interregnum. This poem is considered one of Marvell's finest and is possibly
the best recognized carpe diem poem in English." From *Wikipedia*, online at
http://en.wikipedia.org/wiki/To_His_Coy_Mistress.

Adam Rothstein

The Shape of Shaping Things To Come

53

F.A.T., *The Free Universal Construction Kit: The Universal Adaptor Brick*, 2012. Image courtesy F.A.T.

A weird commotion outside wakes you up. You peer out the window to see the source of the music and revelry. A group of college kids from the engineering school are smashing all of their furniture in the street. The next day while walking the dog, you see them again. They're sweeping up the pieces of broken housewares, and shoveling it into bags. The next day, it looks like they're moving in again as they carry brand new designer furniture into their house. They do this every month or so.

You are shopping in Ikea, looking for a new end table, and perhaps a rug. Suddenly, uniformed security guards appear and surround a young woman. She is escorted from the store, uneventfully. "Pocket scanner," you hear an employee tell an inquiring couple.

With delighted expectation, your son unwraps his birthday gift. Awe is quickly replaced by disappointment. "Isn't that the one you wanted?" you ask confused, certain that it was the new action

figure, ordered directly from the TV show web site. "Yeah, it's the one," he says cautiously, not looking you in the eyes. "I just forgot that all the accessories would be un-modded on the store version."

3D printed objects, or "physibles" are an incredible example of the mundane aspects of future-weird. They are glitchy-as-fuck, but their shapeshifting effect on our cultural space will inhabit the same metaphysics of street graffiti – appreciated by only a few, truly understood by even less.

A physible is simple. Download a file with information about the shape of an object, or component parts of an object. Use a 3D printing machine that squirts molten plastic, metal or other material to pour you that object, without needing a mold. Or, send the file to a company who will do that for you. These machines simplify the process of fabbing an object, by using a single machine to create parts of nearly anything. Previously, specific injection molds had to be created for each piece, or a welder had to attach pieces by reading a diagram. Now the machine can build the entire piece in one run, with basically zero set-up investment. The investment to produce a single object is nearly nothing – all it takes is the design, and one of these universal printing machines.

This technical evolution is interesting, but the real revolution will be in the changing distribution of fabrication shops that this production shift will create. Fabrication has been sourced wherever the set-up requirements are cheapest, with the production runs made as large as possible. But the technology behind physibles will make short-run fabrication, anywhere, much more preferable. It will eventually be cheaper for a person to fab one object at home, than to buy one of five hundred thousand made in one place and shipped across the world. Physibles will decentralize the Pearl River, and bring China home.

But the technology of physibles doesn't mean much to the consumer. Not any more than the encoding of a MP3 file, or the precise stitch pattern of a handbag. It means something to the person who actually fabs the object, but as a consumer, you'll get your things wherever is cheapest and easiest, just like always. You'll still order things online. Rather than coming from China, perhaps a Chinese company will outsource the design to a fab shop down the street that will hand deliver it to your door. The means of production continue to mean nothing to the end-user: commodity cost is king. Most people want their stuff to just be stuff, and don't care about how it works. Consider the frustration people experience trying to get a PDF to print correctly on a flat sheet of paper. These folks will be filling their cabinets, entertaining their children, and brushing their teeth with physibles every day of their lives without knowing how the object came into existence, or what that means for global distribution networks.

Most people. On the other hand, there will be a new set of object hackers, who will be spending all their free time online, discussing the precise interior dimension ratios of the new set of Target glassware (which, they have discovered, is almost exactly equivalent in volume to a very famous American glass company's 1940 catalog). Their forums will be filled with discussion of the best way to minimize wind resistance on custom bicycle fenders, while still maximizing spray blockage. Drug paraphernalia will be designed for maximum efficiency, with a willing and ready test market. A new hacker vernacular will be filled with implicit understandings of the integrals of surface area and volume, of curves and angles, of phase change curves and stress tolerances. One more set of bright kids will take a hard tangent outward from the common understanding matrix of "mainstream society". But if you're nice to them, perhaps they'll fab you a custom iPhone case for Christmas.

Of course, there will be people who get into this deep. As 3D printers get cheaper and more functional, there will be folks that just can't avoid diving head first into this new physical object magic. Even less people will download physibles from The Pirate Bay than download ebooks, but those who do will shape the world for the rest of us. They will be that hot nozzle, spraying our sense of physical existence into reality according to precisely calculated coordinates.

These physible hackers will crave new material. They'll need stuff to work with and to hack, just like DJs need new tracks to cut up. You'll see weird looking people in stores, fondling new design products. Measuring them. Pointing lasers at them. Taking cell phone photos from multiple angles. Physible hackers' creations will remain on the outskirts, like custom-painted skateboard decks, like underground mixtapes. This marginal domain will have its superstars, its up-and-comers, and its sell-outs. Retro physible hackers will take up woodworking, just to "make something real". You'll be able to tell physible-hackers by their weird stuff. That friend of a friend, whose apartment is filled with contorted lamps and more abstract vases than any 20-something really needs. The girl on the subway platform, with a pair of headphones/cosplay-animal-ears you've never seen on anyone else. The freebox on front lawn of that house with the loud music, that occasionally has bizarre, nearly unusable dishware sticking out of it. Is that dishware? Or is a porcelain hat?

This stuff will stay in the fringes, until it somehow becomes cheaper and more appealing than stuff on the shelf. Then you'll buy modded, open-source objects without realizing it, there being nothing to distinguish them from "real" objects. You'll see modded objects, and never know that you have never seen the original, just like you hear remixes without ever listening to the original song. You'll be told in product reviews to search out the "forked" object via this link, rather than buy the real one on Amazon. You'll click, inquisitively, but the link will be dead. There will be new forms of Digital Rights Management, and new ways around that Digital Rights Management. There will be some amazing innovations in objects that have pretty much been the same for the last one hundred years: pretty ingenious new door stops and mouse traps. A 12 year-old will give a TED talk about how she stumbled upon a new type of eating utensil while doing a homework assignment for some class called "Fab Lab": whatever that is. *Cool Tools* will be shut down by a DMCA notice, for failing to cull links to physibles from their comments threads. None of this will matter to you, unless you know what *Cool Tools* is. [1]

You'll see "cancered objects" [2], or other New Aesthetic [3] artifacts on the surface of physical objects. Whereas once we accepted the blobs and seams left by injection molds without a second thought, we will accept the new characteristics of things that physibles provide without knowing it, as the physical semi-error-states of physibles slowly move from bug to feature.

But the production artifacts won't just be on the surface of the object, in the unique flaws of the actual fab process. Artifacts will grow in our mental conceptions of what things are, and what space is. Our aesthetic sense of negative space will be synonymous to the scattered shot of a 3D scanner's laser beam. Pixelated curves in physical space will form a low-res, "8 Bit" houseware aesthetic. Inset or missing blips in the resolution of the surfaces of our stuff will be a natural aspect of the college student's lifestyle. A physible hacker could navigate this newly crystalizing structure of our cultural space. Given enough coffee or booze, s/he could expound for hours on the means of production and the social implication of various bioplastic distribution networks and recycling schemes. But who would really care? Geeks – am I right? Would the plight of minimum-wage object fabbers using carcinogenic printing materials matter to us any more than the suicide pacts of Foxconn workers?

I'm thinking of this as the "mundane future-weird" because while it's going to be weird, it's also just going to be resolutely more of the same. Does it really matter how any of the thousands of disposable objects that clog our sense of time and space got to be there? Does anyone care about how things came to be, past their ability to move a shiny-new-something from one set of hands to another, and perhaps make a buck in the process? If there is anything truly surprising about the future, it's that we are never really surprised when it finally arrives. Nothing springs from the earth fully formed. Everything comes from somewhere – whether from the nozzle of a 3D printer in a hackerspace, or straight from the endless cycle of "capitalism," whatever that is. Those who know, already know. Those who don't aren't likely to be suddenly shocked out of their current state of mind by a table lamp, even if it is smashed in the street.

Don't be disappointed though. If you really want to see weird, you just have to jump a step ahead. But what about scanning and printing buildings, copying and archiving architecture? What about terraforming? What if the unique drainage contours of a fertile river valley are scanned, and then used to reshape an area destroyed by strip mining, or suffering cataclysmic rainfall increases from climate change? The physible, a file containing the geodetic and topographical information, is beamed to a thousand drone bulldozers. After a week, the land is shaped as easily as using Photoshop's clone-stamp tool on a Google Map. How about plastic surgery? How about internal surgery? Why have your heart, with a family history of disease, when you could have the heart of a person who lived to be one-hundred and five? Let us fab you a new future, from scans of other futures of the past.

But it all becomes academic after awhile. We already do those things as well. We shape the earth, we shape ourselves. We shape space and time. It's just modded neologisms and recycled phrases squirting from the end of the nozzle. The stuff that you fab, ends up fabbing you.

First published on *Rhizome* on March 8, 2012. Available online at
http://rhizome.org/editorial/2012/mar/8/shape-shaping-things-come/.

ADAM ROTHSTEIN is an insurgent archivist and writes about politics, media,
and technology wherever he can get a signal.

Notes

[1] "Cool Tools is a web site which recommends the best/cheapest tools
available. Tools are defined broadly as anything that can be useful. This
includes hand tools, machines, books, software, gadgets, websites, maps,
and even ideas." It was founded by Kevin Kelly in 2000 as an email list, and
turned into a blog in 2003. More info at http://kk.org/cooltools/.
[2] Object cancers are small glitches that would only become visible upon
reprinting, inserted in physibles in the form of watermarks to prevent copying.
Cf. "Object Cancers", in *BLDGBLOG*, February 5, 2012. Online at
http://bldgblog.blogspot.it/2012/02/object-cancers.html.
[3] "The New Aesthetic is a term used to refer to the increasing appearance of
the visual language of digital technology and the Internet in the physical
world, and the blending of virtual and physical. The phenomenon has been
around for a long time but lately James Bridle and partners have surfaced the
notion through a series of talks and observations. The term gained wider
attention following a panel at the SXSW conference in 2012." From Wikipedia,
online at http://en.wikipedia.org/wiki/New_Aesthetic. For more information
about the New Aesthetic, cf. the New Aesthetic Tumblr run by British artist
and designer James Bridle: http://new-aesthetic.tumblr.com/.

Joanne McNeil

A Conversation With Jonathan Lethem

THE ECSTASY OF INFLUENCE

A plagiarism
By *Jonathan Lethem*

All mankind is of one author, and is one volume; when one man dies, one chapter is not torn out of the book, but translated into a better language; and every chapter must be so translated....
—John Donne

LOVE AND THEFT

Consider this tale: a cultivated man of middle age looks back on the story of an *amour fou*, one beginning when, traveling abroad, he takes a room as a lodger. The moment he sees the daughter of the house, he is lost. She is a preteen, whose charms instantly enslave him. Heedless of her age, he becomes intimate with her. In the end she dies, and the narrator—marked by her forever—remains alone. The name of the girl supplies the title of the story: *Lolita*.

The author of the story I've described, Heinz von Lichberg, published his tale of Lolita in 1916, forty years before Vladimir Nabokov's novel. Lichberg later became a prominent journalist in the Nazi era, and his youthful works faded from view. Did Nabokov, who remained in Berlin until 1937,

Jonathan Lethem is the author of seven novels, including Motherless Brooklyn and You Don't Love Me Yet, which will be published in March.

adopt Lichberg's tale consciously? Or did the earlier tale exist for Nabokov as a hidden, unacknowledged memory? The history of literature is not without examples of this phenomenon, called cryptomnesia. Another hypothesis is

that Nabokov, knowing Lichberg's tale perfectly well, had set himself to that art of quotation that Thomas Mann, himself a master of it, called "higher cribbing." Literature has always been a crucible in which familiar themes are continually recast. Little of what we admire in Nabokov's *Lolita* is to be found in its predecessor; the former is in no way deducible from the latter.

Still: did Nabokov consciously borrow and quote?

"When you live outside the law, you have to eliminate dishonesty." The line comes from Don Siegel's 1958 film noir, *The Lineup*, written by Stirling Silliphant. The film still haunts revival houses, likely thanks to Eli Wallach's blazing portrayal of a sociopathic hit man and to Siegel's long, sturdy auteurist career. Yet what were those words worth—to Siegel, or Silliphant, or their audience—in 1958? And again: what was the line worth when Bob Dylan heard it (presumably in some Greenwich Village repertory cinema), cleaned it up a little, and inserted it into "Absolutely Sweet Marie"? What are they worth now, to the culture at large?

Appropriation has always played a key role in Dylan's music. The songwriter has grabbed not only from a panoply of vintage Hollywood films but from Shakespeare and F. Scott Fitzgerald and Junichi Saga's *Confessions of a Yakuza*. He also nabbed the title of Eric Lott's study of minstrelsy for his 2001 album *Love and Theft*. One imagines Dylan liked the general resonance of the title, in which emotional misdemeanors stalk the sweetness of love, as they do so often in Dylan's songs. Lott's title is, of course, itself a riff on Leslie Fiedler's

In 2007, novelist Jonathan Lethem published an essay [1] in Harper's ending with a grand reveal: "every line I stole, warped, and cobbled together." The patchwork includes dozens of sources – part of a Steve Erickson novel, something from a Pitchfork review, a quote from an interview with Rick Prelinger. Sandra Day O'Connor and Ralph Waldo Emerson are stitched in too.

"The Ecstasy of Influence", now the title of his recent collection of writings [2], often addresses the process of integrating and "cobbling together" ideas and culture to make something new. Yet, stories Lethem relates of hosting "mailing parties" for the Philip K Dick Society or working in a bookstore seem like snapshots from pre-digital age. Recently I talked with the author about our rapidly dematerializing culture as well as appropriation as an art practice.

JM: Have you ever tried to imagine what kind of career path you would have had without a culture of physical objects?

JL: It's really interesting because I do think of the procedural experience of having to dig, having to find out what, let's say, all of those names in the back of Greil Marcus' *Stranded* were [3]. Now when I read that collection, I see it put together like his esoteric nod to the history of rock and roll and like 80 percent of it was terra incognita. I didn't know the names at all, and I couldn't just go skimming around and get a little taste. I had to make each and every one of those things that compelled me – because of the name or his description – a search. I'd have to go find some broken down piece of media, some old vinyl or something, and you know, the delay that inserts, the relationship to time. I spent a lot of time thinking about a culture that wasn't right at hand.

I might envision a given song or movie for five or ten years before I'd lay hands on it at times, and that creates this sort of personal, fictional vision. It's like having a book unread on your shelf and just staring at the jacket or the title or what you've heard about it, and having it emanating all this promise. Books I guess, can still do that, but it's a really peculiar thing for me to think about how I would relate differently.

I mean, I was advantaged. I grew up in New York City. Compared to other versions of access in our generation, I had great access. My parents had a good record collection and really interesting books on the shelves and pointed me to them. There was no quarantine. I was in New York City and there were great repertory houses and I started going to them when I was 14 or 15 years old, just gobbling down some curators' ideas of cinema. I was getting all these versions of importance or interest out of the obscure past or out of other national cinemas. So in that way, it was like I was surrounded. I didn't even think of myself as deprived.

The strange thing that the question sets up is an image of me, or anyone my age, as somehow suffering from a drought. But I wouldn't have, of course, had the comparison. I wouldn't have had any notion that I was lacking materials. I still had to make really complicated priorities for myself because there was so much that seemed so compelling, potentially compelling. And it wasn't too hard to get a hold of it. But I did, in retrospect I did have these kinds of limits and always a physical relationship – a movie theater that smelled a certain way. What it was to go to the Thalia and watch Bunuel films. It's associated for me with the feeling of that lobby and the strange loneliness in that place on a Thursday afternoon and the other people who would be there present or the kinds of record stores where I would look at things or the bookstores and the way the objects themselves felt and became talismanic. And the way my own room was changing if I brought these things! It wasn't like I could close the computer and it would all go away. It was like I was changing my body practically. To just start accruing all this stuff like armor, like an exoskeleton.

JM: I'm sure your consumption of culture now is different though. Do you have a Kindle or an iPad? Are you an ebook reader? I'm sure you have MP3s, at least.

JL: I have a lot of MP3s! I'm going to qualify this in a number of different ways. I've always been a very late adopter. I mean even MP3s, I didn't have them after other people I knew did. Something about me always sort of wants them to become a little more part of the world. It's like I need to believe in them by seeing people form attachments before I make that move. I've got a friend who teases me because he remembers me saying that I would probably never bother with email. I knew a few people who were doing it and it just didn't seem that appealing to me. Now I'm ten years into an unbelievable promiscuous emailing binge that will never end. So I've been a late adopter a lot of times with tech. I wrote novels on an electric typewriter after it was possible to begin writing prose on computers. I just wasn't quite there. I wasn't ready to make a move from something that felt very important and material and personal to me. So who knows what I might do later on, but I've never read anything on a Kindle and I haven't even really had an iPad or a Kindle in my hands. The nearest I've been has been in the seat beside me in an airplane when I feel smug because they have to stop reading when the announcement goes out and my book is still open.

I think as a writer about the shape and heft of a book. And so I think the reason I am attached to reading them is I'm writing into that form. For better or worse, I still think of where physically my hands would be turning the pages. Feeling, oh, maybe now I'm ten pages from the end. And so some of those things are sacrificed in the Kindle.

Also, the kind of doubling back that I do as a reader seems very fundamental to pages. I'll keep my finger sometimes even three or four pages width in two places in a book. Because I'm interested in doing a doubling. It's very much a part of the physical object to me.

JM: It's almost like screens in that sense that you have the multiple views at once.

JL: It is, yeah. But the other thing, the conversation that I don't ever hear – the single object versus the single object; Kindle versus the book. I have this very, very intense, lifelong relationship to the roomful of books. And the idea of walls of these objects. Rooms that are given over to them – libraries, bookstores, or personal collections. And I don't hear this description very often, that even if somehow they could make a Kindle that you held and it would be like a book in every regard as you held it – the paper would feel papery and the weight would feel weightful and so forth, you'd hit refresh and it would be a different book – but you only have the single object. But I actually feel that I would be even more hard-pressed to give up these kinds of rooms and the sense of orientation with a spatial field of books. That's so crucial, so formative, for me.

JM: I had a funny experience the other day where I was waiting for a bus that was very late and my book was out of batteries.

JL: I don't want my books to get out of batteries.

JM: You probably know this – I want to say there is a writer who travelled around with a suitcase full of books. There are probably a lot of them but there's one who is known for this.

JL: I think most famously – Somerset Maugham writes about his steamer trunk full of books that had to go everywhere with him. I think more than one person has bragged of this or confessed this. That's another thing – it's funny because, ironically, if someone wants to have the dummy argument with you: "Oh wait, you don't have a Kindle yet?" Their surest foot forward, the one where they think they have won the argument before it has even begun is they'll say "for travel." "Come on, for travel. You must."

But in fact, one of my most precious interactions with my books is when I'm going for a trip that is long enough that I don't need just one. When I'm going for a two- or three-week trip, you're not relocating your office; you're not shipping a whole bunch of stuff ahead of you, you're really just packing exactly that range of things you might want to read. And it is a kind of visualizing of a grouping of things that you want to have with you, and then packing them and having them with you. That has got a lot of charm, actually. Sure, I would save space with just the Kindle, but even that, I'll express a little bit of resistance on. There is something about taking the cluster of three or four books and visualizing I'm going to read this one, start it off, but then I'll have this particular one waiting. I won't have very many choices. I'll just have the ones I've brought. There's something so intense and clarifying about that selection.

JM: Because you consume so many books and films and a lot of other things, how do you think that comes out in your original work? How is that blended into something? I'm thinking of Richard Nash's project *Small Demons* [4] – what it does is it cross-references the metadata. So for example, with *Empire of the Sun* it will show all the movies that are referenced there. It will show all the actresses; it will show all the proper nouns as images from Google Search or another service. I feel like your books are probably covered with a lot of interesting references as well. Is that something that you think a lot about in terms of making the work time-sensitive?

JL: There's a number of concepts that I grapple with frequently and sometimes in conversations that are frustrating to me because the terms are circumscribed. But this won't be that. To take the simplest thing first – and I'll offer what may be by now kind of a rote defense of temporal references – David Foster Wallace has that great quote which I stole and injected as a paragraph of *The Ecstasy of Influence* essay, where he is talking about being in a writing class with someone who he calls "the gray eminence." And the gray eminence is criticizing his characters' uses of recent technology or references to recent cultural things as not being timeless enough and wrecking the fiction for posterity or for anything but a kind of immediate reader. And then Wallace sort of reflects on how this guy's fiction is of course full of all his personal stack of technologies – cars, telephones, and mimeograph machines or whatever it might be, and all sorts of cultural things that seem quite natural and embedded in the texture of mimetic reality to this guy. And he realizes this is just generational anxiety, anytime that you are getting this pressure.

The fact is, fiction is made up of reference. Obviously, you could make a scale and put a Kafka parable on one side, and you could have Thomas Pynchon on the other side or somebody, Mark Leyner, I guess, or somebody who exfoliates into innumerable culturally sticky arrows pointing in all directions. But most of us are in the range in-between. And it's okay. It's just okay. It's what it is. You do this. You make reference. In fact even Kafka, you find there are things that are immediate to his culture. Scholarship is endlessly proving that he was looking at a particular film or something before he wrote. So he may not wear it on his sleeve, but it happens anyway. We're not abstract expressionist painters. We're using language and we're using culture and narrative and human life. We're immersed in stuff and some of it is often wanting to be referential in a pretty specific way. And if you read Dickens, in fact, the texture of his London is all over – the advertising jingles of his day and street names and so forth. And so at some point I just inoculated myself against that anxiety totally.

To widen the framework to the question that really engages me and that for me is a consuming one – well, I just feel like I am cursed with, in a way, an autism about the injunctions or the inhibitions against, first, knowing when you're borrowing and, second, saying so. I just always can tell the flow of other people's rhythms – spoken, written – the flow of musical or filmic echoes into my work is constant. It's tangible, it's enjoyable, and I don't really understand how I could be expected to somehow play at barricading myself against what happens, which is that you make work out of everything that's at hand. Everything inside yourself is eligible and you usually find that eventually you're using most everything that's in there and you use your friends, yes, and your family and people you never got to know, but you heard them say a line in a restaurant or on television when they were a bystander at a bicycle-pedestrian accident or anything. You use characters from other people's fiction. It all gets in there. It all gets transformed. That's also automatic. The blessing and the reason to take in so much is to see it all transformed. And to see how that unifies your work and makes it personal and makes it fundamentally authentic.

I'm not really interested in worrying about divisions of originality versus sourcing or appropriations. I'm interested in the authentic, vivid, remarkable, and intimate. I want to feel the grain of another person's intelligence and voice and expressivity and their own version of this kind of helpless intensity that that they feel in the face of existence. Just being alive, being subjective, living in a world of humans and their stuff. It's overwhelming and so the art I like and the art I try to license myself to make doesn't pretend to have control over that plenitude, but to just abide, just to be inside it and make something. And if you do that, it guarantees what other people might tend to call originality, but I just avoid the word as much as I can. What they mean by originality is that it just feels intensely real and persuasive and necessary. Personal. Not borrowed in a pointless way.

JM: This reminds me of what Simon Reynolds said at the Goethe Institute a few months back. He was commentating on your essay, *The Ecstasy of Influence* and said that the power of that essay was that you're a novelist known for your originality.

69

Were you aware when you wrote it that it would perhaps come across with more authority coming from you as opposed to someone better known for appropriation in his or her work?

JL: First of all, I am honored that Simon was making this remark, and I swelled to hearing anything like this, but, at the same time I sort of want to play at it and say, "Well I may be known for my originality but, I am not known to myself for my originality." Because, I think of my work as super-extensively sourced and I am really going to be insistent on that. Mostly when people see things as original it means they don't know where they came from. It's kind of that simple but, I don't mean that as "Whoa snap, I can't believe you said that, it's so mean." I mean that I don't know where everything came from either, who does? Things come from places largely and then they get recombined or spun or give a different flavor or different emphasis. I can think of a 100 precursors to almost anything I've done and honestly, sometimes you don't stand on the shoulders of giants. Sometimes you stand on shoulders of dwarfs. There are things that I thought. "Oh, that's minimally interesting, but I think there is something about it I can improve and turn into my own." Other times you are conscious of a series of precursors that no one else would ever spot or think about unless you pointed it out – and I'm that dope who is always pointing it out. For originality is really truly an overrated concept except as a nice form of praise. It's like you want to say "wow." It's a way of saying wow.

What I think Simon is trying to say – I'll backtrack a little bit. I've come of age inside the family of a painter who'd been trained in an era of modernism. He'd studied in Paris and then Columbia. My father's first attempt was to be an abstract impressionist but he was a little too late to be a modernist. So he, along with everybody else, went back to figuration and he arrived at a style, which in a very, very loose way, you could say he was an early post-modern painter. I don't think he identifies with it. That word very few people do comfortably. He devised a kind of a figurative expressionism and started using some collage elements and this was the beginning of the 60's. He taught me about the twentieth century and I couldn't help noticing that just about every single art gesture except that of the abstract expressionists was a collage gesture. The cubists, the dadaists, the pop artists, everybody was grabbing stuff. Ad Reinhardt and Mondrian even. You just saw that art was made of appropriations and references in a very enthusiastic way. Simultaneously, I was being schooled at the low end, you might say, by Bugs Bunny – Warner Bros cartoons, which were exhilarating. One of my earliest private aesthetic experiences, because it wasn't confirmed – my parents didn't hand that over to me. They did a lot of great stuff. And it was all jokes about references outside the frame, many of which I didn't understand but, I liked them anyway and this was really important. I could think that it is very funny for Bugs Bunny to pretend to be Edward G. Robinson without having seen an Edward G. Robinson movie. I could think that *The Barber of Seville* sequence was hilarious without knowing what *The Barber of Seville* opera sounded like. And, in fact, there are lots of even more temporal things. They make jokes about contemporary news events and those cartoons and stuff that has been forgotten, lost completely. And that just made me feel – ok, this kind of embedded referentiality and borrowing and parody within powerfully expressive, in this case, powerfully ludicrous artwork – good! It's all good. I like it.

And this carried over to one of my earliest and most formative literary experiences, which was Lewis Carroll, and I still think there's almost no text as central for me in becoming a writer as the two Alice books. You can't help noticing, even at eleven or twelve, those things are loaded with all sorts of arch-borrowings and references and pastiches and parodies. And then you could also get the Martin Gardner *Annotated Alice* [5] and find out what a lot of those things are. And it was, again, all good. So from high and from low, I was just like, this is what it's about. It was in my body. It was basic.

So when I then found myself in an atmosphere where people were putting up barricades or quarantines or expressing this anxiety that you aren't meant to be so influenced or so referential or that you better temper it or sublimate it or pretend not to be, even when you are, I just didn't get it at all. And, again, my organic aesthetic response was right there with me when sampling first emerged in music. When I heard the first Public Enemy record or whatever that moment was and I was like, "Crazy quilt of sonic collage. That's music. Great music. I'm all for that."

I had no reservations and I had to really always work not to think that people who were protesting or, you know, made indignant about it, "That's not music" or something were not in total bad faith because I just thought, "It's you versus the entire 20th Century, dude. Everything points to this. How could you possibly misunderstand?"

And when I then also developed my specific ambition to be a writer and to work in this arena of narrative and fiction, which is in some ways very staid. The art form has some very staid elements and the world of its reception has a lot of, let's say, pre-modern biases still floating around. And I realize, writers and novelists are among the most not-yet-up-to-speed on appropriation. I'm not just in an average arena here. I'm in a real retrograde zone.

Well, it amused me. It didn't necessarily seem really important or my big problem because the kind of reference I do actually doesn't, unless you point to it, you know, I'm not going to get sued. I'm never going to get sued for what I do, but when the arguments began to emerge from what we would, I guess, pretty much agree simply to call "the copyleft", right? And then suddenly there's really energetic stuff going on. Lawrence Lessig and, artists like Negativland, who are provocateurs, or The Tape-beatles [6]. Also the arguments that emerged, the legal arguments and the legal feats for someone like Hank Shocklee. Suddenly it was politicized on both sides and the digital age led to the backlash. The very industry that, of course, had digitized their entire catalog suddenly didn't want you to use it that way.

And there was a political discourse. It was very compelling to me. I knew which side I was on very definitely, and when I listened to it, I didn't hear my own voice. I heard two different kinds of voices, both of them very persuasive and appropriate in their very different ways. One was like the, legal intervention like Lawrence Lessig, Siva Vaidhyanathan. People who were lending their brilliance to shoring up the rights of artists from the outside, not working artists. And they would tend always to offer a kind of nuanced or a pragmatist position about ideas of copyrights, for instance. And then there were artists, but the artists were all tending to the avant-garde side of say, Cory Doctorow. They were provocateurs. They were interested in web-based activities specifically, for the most part, or digital activities. They were making work often that was defiantly illegal or provoked cultural norms about appropriation and they were strident. They were funny, strident, they were pissed off, they were irreverent, and this was also very persuasive to me and appropriate, but I didn't hear about someone speaking passionately in the copyleft perspective from the middle of a career, of a normative regular kind of, "I've got a publisher. It's a big publisher. I make my living by copyrights. My work doesn't get me sued so I have no personal stake in somehow giving myself more elbow room. You know, I'm not in Hank Shocklee's position or something on being on the verge of losing my tools."

And yet, I wanted to say, even for one such as me who could just placidly go along ignoring this whole fuss, I actually have a very powerful motive for throwing everything I have, rhetorically, passionately, emotionally onto the side of the copyleft, and the reason being that the other side tells a lie about what artists do and how they really think and feel and thrive. And also, there is a risk for every artist of damage being done not just to the ethos of how art is made, but to the actual traditions and behaviors. If more and more people really buy into this image of the Promethean isolated creator who's only legitimate because he invents out of nothing – and it really informs the culture and the laws and the way art is taught and the way art is received – it's propagating a dangerous befuddlement about how we really go about things. We're in a really messy area. We pick stuff up and we fool around with it and it's stuff. It's stuff that's around us. Some of it is owned, in some sense, by someone else and some of it isn't, and sometimes we don't even know, and sometimes we're doing it half consciously. And we must. We must do all of these things. There's no other possibility.

JM: Have you thought about at what point is it maybe ethical to cite someone else for any contributions to your work?

JL: There are all sorts of ethical judgments we can make about these behaviors. You know, morality is the grave level of life and death and ethics is the next layer up. Some of these I would even put at another thinner layer of civility or courtesy. You can make lots of judgments about ethics, civility, courtesy, etc., but it's really, first of all, important to specify this is not actually a moral area. Even though people will express enormous amounts of indignation and righteousness about it, these are not generally life and death matters. Very, very often they're much, much less like matters of livelihood than people make them out to be. It's very hard to hurt someone else's livelihood by plagiarizing them for instance. It's just about impossible to even in the most aggressive and pernicious way, to take away, unless you literally have access to their computer and you steal their draft before they can publish it, under your own name. It's just really hard to do anything. It could be totally yucky, but it's not really actually very easy to make much of a dent in their livelihood. These are not mostly moral matters. These are ethics and norms and matters of courtesy and protocol and so forth. Well yeah, we can make lots of judgments in that zone. I do all the time. I think lots of people do. The really crucial thing to say about those is, when the question comes, just as it did from you, "is there a point?" To say in each specific case, yes, there is, but the generalization still works. You can't say, "So here's how we're going to do it." It's actually always very individual, I think.

When I'm challenging people to think about it this way, the suggestion I always use is that we talk about music because people can really latch onto these feelings in music and the reference is usually familiar to everyone. Also there's a lot of transparency in that realm. There are sort of two primary axes on which we make the individual judgment. One is: degree of transformation and the other is degree of transparency and or citation. In other words, how much do they really make something different out of what they appropriated? And how much did they make it easy to see that there was someone else's gesture behind their own? Every single appropriating gesture can be looked at on both of these axes and sometimes something will score very high on one but score very poorly on the other or sometimes it's a mixture. So take my dummy examples: Willy Dixon, great blues man, was radically appropriated by Led Zeppelin and for a long time this struck people as a kind of hideous example of kind of exploitative appropriation because they took his name off the songs until they were literally sued into putting his name back on the songs. Because they were fabulously wealthy white guys running around the world having sex with groupies, while he was like and old black guy, who we tend to sentimentalize as the victim in this scenario and I think there's every reason that we have those kinds of feelings about it. It scored terribly poorly on the transparency – they're unbelievably world famous, he's not a household name.

They specifically deleted his name from his own compositions. Just egregious gesture on the level of transparency or citation. On the other hand, on the level of transformation, those Led Zeppelin songs do not sound like Willy Dixon to me. They took his composition and they made something very different and that difference was so earth shattering. First of all, it made them wealthy and it changed music forever, the whole genre of music was basically piled on top of this gesture, so it was a totally high score on transformation. They did not just play those songs the way Willy Dixon did. The transformation was staggering, in fact that's probably why they thought they could get away with the appropriation. They didn't seem to have a relationship anymore to some people. So that's one where you have a very high score on one side. It's like the fiddler crab image, the transformation is organic and the claw of transparency, terrible. Let's flip it, lets find an opposite example: Paul Simon goes to Africa and he hears some stuff he likes and he puts out this record, which if you've never heard any African music, ever in your life, it's the most radical, mind blowing, extraordinary record anyone's ever heard called *Graceland*. It changes everything. How could this be? What are these sounds? They're making my head spin! If you know anything about African music, especially if you know quite a lot about African music, it was like, that is so wearisome. He basically took Soweto sound and he laid a thin layer of neurotic upper west side Jew stuff on top of it. It's just like Paul Simon nattering away over the top of African music. So the claw of transformation very poor, very inadequate for a lot of people. But on the other hand, what did he do? He not only credited these guys, he put them in a van and he drove around the country and he played on stage with them. Right beside them. The claw of transparency is the most amazing gesture ever. He was just like, "Hey, don't look at me, look at these great African guys!" It was like if Willie Dixon was the lead singer of Led Zeppelin. So he has reversed it completely.

Now, in an ideal world every appropriative gesture would have Led Zeppelin-level transformation with Paul Simon-level transparency. That would be great. We don't always get that. We often get some imbalance or some weird mixture or we're not sure. Also, we're not always sure. Sometimes things come also from somewhere else. Or there's a common denominator or whatever. It's like it's not always so clear-cut. So you have to look at each and every gesture and decide how you feel about it. You can't make a law about it.

But I'll add even on to that, that there are also really important differences from medium to medium, even in the capacity to cite. T.S. Elliott has this appendix to *The Wasteland* where there are all these citations. We'll put aside the fact that probably no one ever bothers to read that. But it's there. He tried. It's right there. But if a painter makes a canvas, it does not have room for footnotes on it. And a lot of art, the form doesn't invite the same kinds of embrace of transparency. The specific gestures just don't work. So what do you do? There might be follow-up. You could speak in an interview, you could make a gesture. But you know what? Not everyone wants to do that. Not everyone wants to be interviewed about their work at all. They want to just make it. And that's okay.

This is one of these places where I just want to keep reminding people that art is not principally in the moral sphere. It's not really about do we feel like this is a good purpose or not. It's more about – Holy shit! What's that? And that is what it's for. And how does it make us feel? The ethics and even the morals is mostly about what happens inside of us on meeting it. Which is why, ironically, we are so prone to feeling betrayed by the artist in some way. Because the art does something so extraordinary to us that then we find out some detail. "Oh! He stole that from Willie Dixon." "Oh! He beat his wife." "Oh! He picks his nose in public." "Wait a minute. He made that thing that changed my life. This is incongruent. I don't like it!" That's why we get so betrayed by the knowledge of appropriations, because we're holding art to this very weird standard where it is actually about us. It's about our own lives. It's not about the artist's life. Sometimes we want to be fooled, too. It's silly that people can be so complicated, but then again we don't have any other model. And a lot of us want to be fooled at the same time we get angry that we're fooled. We want the artist to be a kind of Houdini who does magic tricks. And then we simultaneously want to find out that it's an esoteric, comes from an esoteric place where we could never understand how the magic was made. And we want the cards to be turned over so we can understand and make the person seem humble and normal and like us. And then we get angry at them for just being a normal humble person. So what we want is very problematic.

First published on *Rhizome* on April 26, 2012. Available online at
http://rhizome.org/editorial/2012/apr/26/jonathan-lethem/

JOANNE MCNEIL (http://joannemcneil.com) is the former editor of *Rhizome*. She was a 2012 USC Annenberg / Getty Arts Journalism fellow. Her writing has appeared in *Modern Painters*, *Wired UK*, *Frieze*, *The LA Times*, the *Paris Review Daily*, *The Boston Globe*, *n+1*, and other web and print publications.

Notes

[1] Jonathan Lethem, "The Ecstasy of Influence. A Plagiarism", in *Harper's Magazine,* February 2007. Online at http://harpers.org/archive/2007/02/the-ecstasy-of-influence/.
[2] Jonathan Lethem, *The Ecstasy of Influence. Nonfictions*, etc., Doubleday, New York 2011.
[3] Greil Marcus (Ed.), *Stranded. Rock and Roll for a Desert Island*, Da Capo Press 2007.
[4] Online at www.smalldemons.com.
[5] Martin Gardner, *The Annotated Alice: The Definitive Edition*, W. W. Norton & Company, New York 1999.
[6] "The Tape-beatles (also known as Public Works) are a multi-media group that formed in Iowa City in December 1986. [...] Beginning with analog tape recorders, and later expanding to include digital technology and film media, the group has used collage techniques to create works that challenge the notion of intellectual property." From *Wikipedia*, online at http://en.wikipedia.org/wiki/The_Tape-beatles.

80

John Powers

Image of
Democracy:
Why I Want
to Build
Nine Freedom
Towers
in Tiananmen
Square

John Powers, *Proposal for Tiananmen Square*, 2012. Courtesy the artist

"What happened at 9/11 of course changed the scale of all this... It became an issue about fear, and our horror at looking, as I did, out of our windows onto the buildings that were burning. The horror we had in our hearts from this, allowed us... to give up basic freedoms. I'm not just talking about the ones the papers talk about all the time, our democratic and constitutional rights, but in the way we live, the way we block our streets." — David Childs [1]

I am a sculptor, my work is abstract and more often than not described as "post-minimalist." Recently I was asked to contribute a work for a group show in Hong Kong. The curatorial frame of the show is "the ways objects produce space." Rather than contribute a sculpture and hope for some sort of latter-day phenomenological experience between 'object' and 'subject' however, I suggested revisiting an urban design project that I had not worked on for over a decade. Eleven years ago I made a modest proposal to create a series of three massively flat and empty superblocks (two in New York and one in Washington DC). I last showed these proposals as three large architectural site models, just six months before September 11th attacks. Because my proposals seemed to foreshadow the 16 acre gap left in Manhattan's grid, I was urged to revisit the project. I didn't, not because I didn't feel I might have something to contribute, but because I was struck dumb horror. I refused to speak publicly about the project, and although the original show of models had been based on a long essay on the subject of art and public space, I stopped writing for years. Anyone familiar with my blog will understand that this is not my usual MO. But looking back I am now very glad I shut up.

Most of what was said about architecture in the immediate wake of the attacks struck me as tone deaf, some of what was said by artists was unintentionally cruel.

That is not to say I didn't take interest in the site and the conversation around it. I followed the competition to choose a master plan, and still feel Sir Norman Foster's unapologetically hard edged "kissing" chisels were the best of the lot. Most of what I saw and heard however, reinforced the observation that had inspired my proposals in the first place: the widespread inability to know the difference between what can and cannot be changed when it comes to architecture. By wide spread, I mean architects, politicians, critics and loudmouths at parties. Even after Modernist architecture's fall from grace, the expectation is that big challenges must be addressed by massive projects, and that symbolic meaning trumps straight talk (observe Libeskind vs Foster).

While I sympathized with architect's desire to respond to the attacks, I did not understand their responses. Architecture isn't a symbol (that was the hideous confusion the attackers made), it is an expression; a concrete expression of an idea, an ethic, a desire. Modernists plazas are often characterized as "fascist" – the idea being that they are symbolic projections of power. Architects seldom, if ever, discuss lawns, park benches, or flower arrangements as expressions of power. Looked at as concrete ethical expressions, rather than symbols, we can begin to see these things for what they are: impediments, barriers, place holders, and dividers.

I: Double Zero

For the show in Hong Kong I ended up showing recreations of my three original counter-proposals, and a fourth proposal that has been gestating for almost a decade, but has suddenly taken on new relevance. I proposed building nine "Freedom Towers" arranged in a tight grid formation and completely occupying the available open space of Tiananmen Square.

A decade after I proposed paving flat large portions of New York and DC, I want to "occupy" Tiananmen Square with a formation of Freedom Towers. These may seem like two very different projects and two very different political contexts, but in fact they are the same. In 2001 I was suggesting that we had lost an important variety of public space and that our cities and our republic were lessened by that loss. That in the 40 years since the civil rights and anti-war protests of the 1960s American authorities have altered the landscape of our cities – through changes in the rules that concerning public assembly (a process Naomi Wolf calls "overpermiticisation" [2]), but also through bricks and mortar construction. Our public space has been "developed" out of existence.

In the wake of the massive protests in Wisconsin, the "Arab Spring," and the Occupy movement in New York (and everywhere else), it feels important to once again raise the question of public space as a built environment. Rather than continue to argue that we build a new kind of space here, I am suggesting that we imagine what it would mean if we exported our current development schemes to other countries; to imagine them as the work of foreign regimes. What if the National WWII Memorial, with its heroic Speerian colonnade, sunken plaza, and ground-covering fountain, had been built in Tahrir Square rather than midway between the Lincoln Memorial and the Washington Monument? How would we feel if Russian authorities were to announce the construction of a large Frank Gehry designed Guggenheim be built over, Bolotnaya Square, the site of last December's ballot-rigging protests in Moscow?

To mashup SOM's Freedom Tower and China's Tiananmen Square may, at first glance seem arbitrary, but it isn't. Both New York's Ground Zero and Beijing's "Zero Point" are symbolically loaded sites. Non-mainland Chinese associate Tiananmen with the 1989 pro-democracy protests, but for the Chinese it was already a site loaded with meaning when protesters chose that space to take their stand. In his book *Remaking Beijing*, the author Wu Hung describes the formation of Chinese end of this symbolic East-West axis:

"An unlikely coalition of left-wing Chinese architects, Soviet specialists and Western-trained urban planners of a modernist bent, argued that the capital could fully realize its symbolic potential only by locating the government in traditional Beijing. A crucial argument made by this second group was that, because the country's founding ceremony took place in Tiananmen Square, this local should logically

be the center of new Beijing... By relocating 'zero' to Tiananmen Square, the birthplace of the People's Republic, the city would acquire a new identity and a vantage point for its architectural restructuring. Beijing's centre of gravity would automatically shift southward, and the avenue running east-west through the square would become its new axis." [3]

Hung's book discusses what he calls "soft monuments", large scale flower arrangement and other temporary displays. Unlike a "'hard monument' from the previous era that commemorated history and demanded faith, a 'soft monument' of the 1990s and 2000s is deliberately short-lived and goal specific." Now according to Hung, the intention is to displace dissent, depoliticize the space: "Instead of empowering the Chinese people to carry out political or military campaigns against domestic and foreign enemies, images in the Square now express citizens' happiness and unification." In other words, the world's largest public square is now inhospitable to protesters due to strategically arranged flower displays.

The Chinese could learn something from the public/private partnership of American real estate developers and political authorities. One World Trade Center, or Freedom Tower, is the office building replacing the site's fallen Twin Towers, and the latest example of American public/private political double talk – an expression of freedom that is in fact a commercial property where employers and landlords have final say on what will and won't be permitted, what can and cannot be said. Additionally, the building itself is a fortress; an architecture of fear embedded within an urbanism of political self-loathing.

In 2007 the architect of the Freedom Tower, David Childs, gave a talk appropriately titled "Buildings and Fear." I attended because I wanted to know how an architect who had designed a skyscraper built over a 200'x200'x200' cubic volume of uninhabitable bomb-proof cement base, dubbed a "Freedom Tower", would explain himself. I was impressed. Childs turned out to be a smart and self-reflective designer. Although he justified his disguising the building's fortified nature with a façade of "prismatic" glass because the glass would act as a kind of sensor if a blast did occur... Which seemed a bit slippery to me; what impressed me is what he said about the post-9/11 culture of cement barriers and security booths:

"I'm chairman of the Commission of Fine Arts, and I'm very much worried about what's going to be happening to our image of democracy... you can imagine of course right after 911 all this kind of temporary facilities went up but it wasn't very long until the final ones came into place, and they're not much better... So this is a real problem of how we can control this and I found to my surprise that the leaders, the head undersecretaries would come before us and they were reluctant, when we would say "Well, can't you design this in a way so that you don't see it?" And well, in fact, many of them wanted to see it. It was a status symbol. If your agency got more of this kind of junk out in front of it you were obviously more important, and so they didn't want to do it. They really thought you should see it. And this is an attitude that many of the people trying to deal with securities and cities have. And by the way I should say that many of the consultants that we work with are more than reasonable. But many are also fear mongers. They say that we have to do this kind of closing down in order to make it safe, and in order to make it safe it must look safe. So it's not a question of hiding things as probably more expense, but just showing the kind of structures that you put up front to block car combs, and other things, or to look menacing in themselves." [4]

The idea of this mashup dates back to the decision to hold the Olympics in Beijing. There was a well-founded anxiety that the Chinese authorities would take the opportunity to build the "Olympic Village" in Tiananmen Square – thereby making a large-scale protest impossible to effect. While that never came to pass no one could predict the massive restructuring of the city that did take place. In addition to heroic structures by International Starchitects that now dot the city, 100,000 families were relocated to make way for new construction for the Games (see Brazilian Games).

The opportunity to show in China, the fact that the Freedom

Tower is nearing completion, but also the fact that the weather is warming and we can expect fresh round of protests, gave this shelved project new relevance for me. However, the true genesis of this project, of these concerns, dates back to my earliest political memories.

II: SHAME

My father tells a story about a friend of his, who, during the 1960s would drive around with an "all-purpose protest sign" in the trunk of his car, so that whenever he happened on a protest he could easily join the crowd, no matter what the subject of the protest happened to be. His sign simply read "SHAME." I remember hearing the story as a kid, and finding it confusing. I got what my father wanted me to get: I understood why his friend's solution was funny and smart. The part of the story that was confounding was the idea of protests being something you might just "happen upon" while out for a drive.

I knew immediately what my Dad's friend's sign would have looked like – a stick of wood with a large card stapled to it. I could imagine what my dad's friend might have looked like: either a well-groomed black man in a suit or a slovenly youth with long hair and silly cloths. As a child I was familiar with protests only through historical footage of the civil rights and anti-war movements I would have seen on TV. I don't have a single memory of ever having randomly driven past a protest of any kind. My father explained that they used to happen all the time. That people had been more active – once upon a time, in the "60s" – but not any more. As for why, I never got a straight answer from my father or anyone else when I was growing up. Things had once been one way and now they weren't that way anymore.

In high school, I followed a group of friends to a protest (No

Nukes, I think). I remember dressing up. I didn't have long hair, but wanted to show I was "radical" or at the very least "committed" – I think I wore a white bandana, maybe all white. I'm not really sure. The image is more an abstracted feeling of embarrassment, than any clear picture. My friends took me to stand with a small crowd outside a nondescript fence. It was lame. I knew that this was not how it was supposed to be. This is not how it had been for my father when he marched in Selma Alabama with Martin Luther King, or for his friend, who marched with everybody else. Something was missing, something in me, and the people around me; it was a disheartening realization because I had no idea what it was that missing.

Five or six years later, I was hitchhiking down Highway 101 from Seattle. I got as far as San Francisco when the Rodney King verdict was handed down and the LA riots began. Rather than wait out the unrest in SF (where smaller, less spectacular, riots had broken out), I decide to continue slowly hitchhiking down coast, camping and avoiding trouble. It was a dumb plan, but I was lucky. I didn't get into any big trouble, but I was luck enough to have a little trouble find me.

I had hardly gotten out of San Francisco when I was picked up by two young political activists who were rushing down to LA to see what "good," if any, could come from the confusion (they worked with a group that spoke to inner city youths about environmental issues in relation to income and race – good guys). They convinced me I should go down with them and see what was happening. The three of us talked politics the whole way down the 5. I ended up arriving in LA the second night of the riots. We could see the fires as we headed into the city.

I've always wondered what those guys did when they got there, but "... something something about a girl," we parted ways that night. I spent a few days moving around LA by myself on foot, observing the city in lock down. I remember finding it interesting that in a city dominated by cars, the police were able to contain and close down the possibility of riots by closing all public parking. Without a place to park their cars Angelinos couldn't congregate in large enough numbers to intimidate the police.

The next major stop on my trip (being stranded in Barstow doesn't count) was Austin where I stayed with a young Palestinian architect and his wife, an American born political organizer. These friends, both politically active students at University of Texas, were keenly aware of architectural space and protest. They were very interested to hear what I had seen in LA. I told them about the parking, and they told me how in the 1960s students at UT in Austin had gathered in large open spaces on campus, formed into large masses of protestors – too large to be controlled by police – and once these masses had formed, they moved.

Adjacent to campus, and politically far more symbolically potent, is the Texas State Capital. There, at the more politically loaded symbolic space of the Capital "steps," the protestors were able to make their voices heard and their anger felt. My hosts explained how, in the intervening years, the campus had been altered with plantings, benches and berms; impediments that to made it impossible to gather large groups. The lack of a safe and unrestricted open space to 'build mass' made it much harder, if not impossible, to create the 'mass movement' needed to overcome the authorities' understandable desire not to allow protests on their steps. I never considered decorative plantings and benches as anything other than a positive addition to the urban landscape. I now saw them as subtracting from public space – as a division that acted to reshape what could and couldn't happen within public space.

My friends told me that UT's quad wasn't the exception; it was the rule. That since the great campus uprisings of the 1960s quads all around the country had been divided by plantings, earthworks, and hardened features. Likewise American cites had altered public spaces and rules for who could use them and how. The small, lame, and obviously ineffectual protests I had taken part in – even when the stakes were high, as in the case of the first Gulf War – had been engineered to be lame.

I have never taken part in a riot, or, at that time, even a large protest, but I did know what it felt like to move with a large crowd. I had run through the empty streets of the Loop after a Fourth of July fireworks display with a thousand other drunk and high Chicagoans (awesome). I'd slam danced at rock festivals, and moved as an unstoppable body with hundreds of others at sporting events and concerts. I knew how empowering those experiences had been. Those memories stand out above my day-to-day life, they are still exciting to think about years later. So I could imagine how much more potent it would be, had they taken place within the context of a political protest – that those sorts of feelings of power must have supercharged the large protests I had watched in PBS documentaries growing up.

As a teenager in the 1980s I heard a lot of stories about the glory days of the 1960s. The moral of those stories always seemed to be that giants had once walked the earth, and that my friends and I were a diminished race of weaklings. The young people of the past were manifestly more engaged than my generation; my peers and I lacked some essential part (spine, heart, spirit) that our elder's had somehow had in abundance.

The story my friends in Austin told me was different, it pointed to the fact that my friends and I hadn't lacked some ineffable quality, but that the conditions on the ground had change. We weren't radical as a group because we weren't given the space to move *en mass*. To feel empowered as a group, to be physically radicalized by the feeling of standing up to an authority and seeing that the authority could be swayed, or, if need be, *physically* intimidated. The LA riots reordered the ways I looked at cities, especially public spaces. Rather than work towards a healthier body politic, American authorities had altered the body to make it easier to control. I was born into an intentionally hobbled commonweal.

III: The Rhetoric of Power

In 1995 I moved to New York to study art. One of the concerns, I learned, that had shadowed minimalist art during the 1960s is that those plain gray plywood boxes degraded aesthetics. That there was a danger that once we, the public, began accepting those "objects" as art in museums, what was to stop us from looking at cement blocks on city streets as art as well? In 1966, the sculptor Robert Morris observed: "The total space is hopefully altered in certain desired ways by the presence of the object. It is not controlled in the sense of being ordered by an aggregate of objects or by some shaping of the space surrounding the viewer." And asked: "Why not put the work outside and further change the terms?"[5]

As I studied art and learned about the sometimes dry, abstract, and even algebraic ways the space around minimalist art has been thought of (I am not referring to Morris here, who's sardonic and smart writings I admire, but a lot of his peers and countless imitators who took themselves far more seriously). I was observing the qualities of space in the city around me. Shortly after arriving in New York I walked past a small protest near Washington Square. The protesters, who numbered in the dozens, had been hemmed into to small pens by the police. While many of the kids seemed to have dressed for the part, no one carried a placard or brandished a bull horn like the protests I had grown up watching on public television documentaries. I remember thinking that they didn't have the room needed to be truly radicalized; that mass movements require both greater mass than they were allowed and greater movement than they were allowed.

My interest in minimal art might have been a passing phase in my development had it not been for an essay called "Minimalism and the rhetoric of Power" by the feminist art historian Anna Chave [6]. It is a remarkable and deeply critical piece of writing, and unlike the essays I read that defended and justified minimalism in terms of phenomenological encounters, and alienating confrontation, Chave's ideas made sense. Rather than surround the work with an intellectual Rube Goldberg device (phenomenology) she "interrogated" the associations made by artists to images of power – many of them violent and cruel.

Chave isn't perfect. She was harshly critical of the minimalists on a personal level, to a degree I find unfair. She was even mean spirited at times, especially in the case of Robert Morris, who I did my graduate studies with. She also proposed that masculine power can be displaced by some female alternative, which she dubbed "a capacity of nurturance." I find this brand of feminist utopianism as wrong headed as socialist utopianism that set men's minds aflame in the 1920s and 30s, or the brand of neo-liberal utopianism the GOP is so enamored with at the moment. Michel Foucault (who Chave aims to counter) had it exactly right:

"I don't believe there can be a society without relations of power, if you understand them as means by which individuals try to conduct, to determine the behavior of others. The problem is not of trying to dissolve them in the utopia of a perfectly transparent communication, but to give one's self the rules of law, the techniques of management, and also the ethics, the ethos, the practice of self, which would allow these games of power to be played with a minimum of domination." [7]

I met with Chave in early 2001. By then I had been making abstract art for six years, studying with Robert Morris a three of those years, and minimalism, via the Vietnam Veteran's Memorial and the Oklahoma bombing Memorial, had become the semi-official aesthetic of state sponsored mourning in the US. I asked to meet with Chave because, while she argued for an alternative to power I didn't believe in, she was the first and only person I had ever read who spoke clearly about minimalism as I saw it: as powerful and aggressive. Her essay is rightly critical of that power when it is expressed in abusive ways (she really takes Richard Serra and his defenders to task – I often wonder if his gentle and sexy *Torqued Ellipses* aren't a response to Chave criticisms of his earlier work). But I had the chance to ask Chave if, like me, she didn't find that power attractive. "Yes of course I do." She told. "My ambivalence is something most readers don't pick up on." It was clearly something she found regretful.

I asked to meet with Chave in 2001, because that March I was preparing to mount a solo show of three architectural models that made a modest proposal: that minimalist space – the large empty space demanded by minimalist art – if expressed as public space, in dense urban setting, would provide space within which a crowd could form. "Why not put the work outside and further change the terms?" Morris had asked in 1966. Forty years later my reply was to image art as Morris' friend and mentor Tony Smith had described it: as "something vast." And while I did not want to re-imagine power as a capacity for nurturance, I believed Chave provided an answer of sorts. That what was key was to ask, as Chave had: "who speaks to whom, why and for whom." Transferring aesthetic attention from the isolation of the gallery to public space changes the terms from academic concerns of "embodiment" to ethical concerns of power and protest.

IV: Clusterfuck Ethics

The art critic Jerry Saltz calls the "the practice of mounting sprawling, often infinitely organized, jam-packed carnivalesque installations" Clusterfuck Aesthetics. [8] When this aesthetic is put outside, the terms become "disenfranchise" and "marginalize." In March of 2001, I made three counter proposals for three site slated for high profile cultural development: I re-imagined each as a flat, featureless plaza. That year New York City alone had over 5 billion dollars worth of bricks-and-mortar cultural development on the boards. By "bricks-and-mortar cultural development" I mean, the Brooklyn Museum and the Lincoln Center had both proposed much needed renovations (since completed). The Design Museum and the New Museum had respectively announced their aims to rebuild and build fresh (also both since completed). Most spectacularly however, the old Post Office across from Madison Sq Garden on Manhattan's West Side was to become a heroic new entrance to the city: Penn Station reborn, and the Guggenheim had set out to build an enormous Frank Gehry designed clusterfuck (I mean that as an honorific) on the waterfront just below the Brooklyn Bridge. Additionally, Congress had secured funding to build a heroic National WWII Memorial straight out of Albert Speer's note books on the Washington Mall right in the middle of the space that had been occupied by the crowd who listened to Martin Luther King Jr. give his historic "I Have A Dream" speech in 1963.

Like a lot of other ambitious building plans, the Downtown Guggenheim was abandoned in the wake of the September 11th attacks. Evidently the "Moynihan Plan" to rebuild Penn Station is still in play. [9] Unfortunately the funding did not dry up for the WWII memorial (the only one of the three I truly disliked in-and-of-itself). But I couldn't have known that when I made my original counter proposals that March.

The Gehry Museum was part of a mixed public/private development scheme to rejuvenate New York's waterfront. For decades the waterways around Manhattan had been little more than industrial canals and open sewers. But in 1977 Congress passed the Clean Water Act, and by the mid 1990s the city had to concern itself for the first time in over a half century with maintaining wooden piers from infestations of boring worms – a problem that pollution levels had made impossible; for decades the Hudson and East river had been oxygenless deserts where nothing could live. Probably for the first time since prudish Dutch traders settled Manhattan, New Yorkers began seriously considering recreational swimming in the Hudson, and the political response was to ring the island of Manhattan with pay-to-play properties.

The push by authorities, public officials and private developers, was to in-fill; to build a wall of Chelsea Piers and Battery Park City-like developments between New Yorkers and the newly rejuvenated waterways. I believed (and still believe), that a once-in-a-century opportunity to create a vast public space on par with Central Park was being squandered in a fit of neo-liberal profiteering.

In addition to building large-scale models of my counter proposals (two featureless superblocks in NYC, and a decked cubic fountain in DC), I wrote an essay about three public art works in the minimalist vein and I gave a talk for thirty or forty people in the gallery one evening. It's been a while, but as I remember it was a fun night. The audience was mostly architects and artists. The vibe I remember was something along the lines of "Who the fuck are you to opine about urbanism?" My proposals looked an awful lot like retreads of Modernists "windswept plazas" – but I explained that they were carefully different. That those 50's and 60's era spaces had been built on raised plinths with stepped entrances – I used the examples of The Empire State Plaza in Albany, The Lincoln Center, Seagrams Building and the World Trade Center complex as examples of what I was *not* doing.

I wasn't proposing a stage on which to place a building, or a complex of buildings. I was proposing spaces that could be approached from any direction, mounted as easily as one mounts a curb, and contained *nothing*; no trees, no grass, no benches, no fountains or facilities of any sort, just space. I pointed out to my audience that if there were to be a war, there was no place in New York City where a crowd could form in great enough numbers to intimidate police on the street, much less sway hawkish politicians watching from Washington DC. I did my best, but my audience was unmoved, there was some sense that I was being hyperbolic; some sort of Bauhaus Cassandra in an age of Dot Com Pollyannas.

To be fair, every one seemed to have a good time and the discussion was lively, but in March of 2001 war clearly seemed like a ridiculously distant possibility to be worrying over. We had sailed past the millennium's first big crisis (Y2K?), the economy was red hot and our new conservative president was hampered by a questionable election and promised to be ineffective at worst. (One defender lamely claimed "George Bush speaks for the inarticulate.") Our cities didn't need open spaces; if the rumors were true, Dean Kamen had invented a personal flying device that would be unveiled later that year. Who could be bothered to worry about war? (Turned out Dean invented Segways: the millennium's first big fail.)

One audience member spoke up to say we didn't need to protest in person any longer; that large rallies were a thing of the past, an artifact of the 1960s. That we could now make our voices heard on the *internet*. No one was talking about Social Media yet – Virtual Reality was still a really big deal back then. Virtual Presence and Virtual Space were assumed to be around the corner. A smart well-regarded curator told me that because of VR, we would soon be struggling with the "split awareness of being two places at once." I reminded him that we had overcome that problem almost a century ago. And asked him to imagine what he would think if I were to address him in person with the peculiar telephone grammar of "Hello, this is John. Are you there?" (I was too clever by half, as he never showed my work again.)

As a sculptor my mind was going in the opposite direction as those around me. I was already longingly eyeing the technology to out-put the virtual. I didn't want to be a ghost in the machine, I wanted bring digital objects into real space as real material. I still remember being annoyed that the artist Michael Reese used "3D lithography" to make sculptures before I had a chance to. But like everyone else I didn't have the wherewithal to see how the virtual would interface with the actual when it came to political protest, but no one else did either.

The Arab Spring was a series of mass protests that self-organized online (a bit like a digital model – liquid, fast, easy to modify), but manifested themselves physically (point by point, almost like a 3d printer, into a solid mass) as very real protests in very real spaces. It was in those open spaces – Tahrir Square in Cairo, Egypt; Habib Bourguiba Avenue in Tunis, Tunisia; and the Pearl Roundabout in Manama, Bahrain – flat open spaces very much like the ones I had proposed, that whole populations were able to move together as a mass and doing so were radicalized and authorities intimidated. Likewise the Occupy Wall Street protest here in New York had a digital "backend", but owed its success to a group of hardcore protestors who hacked the American Political landscape: rather than form a large mass for a brief protest, they made a small protest last months.

V: Republic Disfigured

Just as the choice of a semi public space turned out to be a stroke of genius because by law is to remain open too the public, the long small protest of Occupy Wall Street was an elegant work-around to the situation Naomi Wolf described after being arrested in October of 2011:

"In 70s America, protest used to be very effective, but in subsequent decades municipalities have sneakily created a web of 'overpermiticisation' – requirements that were designed to stifle freedom of assembly and the right to petition government for redress of grievances, both of which are part of our first amendment. One of these made-up permit requirements, which are not transparent or accountable, is the megaphone restriction." [10]

Wolf is able to clearly identify the changes to what Italo Calvino called the Invisible City [11], but the physical changes, the horror vacui that shaped the material organization of our cities is either so obvious, that it doesn't need to be spoken of, or, like a frog swimming in soup pot, the changes have been so gradual they are less visible than the Invisible.

David Childs, the architect of the Freedom Tower, admits to having misgivings about hardening the offices and residences of our elected officials against attack from elsewhere, because he is aware that this means he is also hardening the structures of our Republic against approach and reproach from within. Who in their right mind would try and visit an elected official's office with a complaint? Unless you are a member of the vanishing small percentage of Americans who are able contribute large amounts to political campaigns (much less than 1% according to Lawrence Lessig), there would be no way to reach them through the mazes of impediments and security checkpoints that Childs helps design. And any attempt to do so would get you put on a no-fly list.

The bomb-proof base, the part of One World Trade Center that I find most offensive, is so offensive not only because it was entirely the product of the worst fear mongering impulses of the Bush years, but because it is also the worst reflection of our contemporary moment. During his talk at Cooper Union, Childs explained that because the WTC had twice been a target of terrorist attacks, security experts had insisted that the design for the building incorporate withstanding a hypothetical 18-wheeler tractor-trailer packed full of C4 explosives being driven up to the base of the tower and detonated.

I don't dismiss the need to protect the site, I am however, totally disgusted by the politics that made it possible to drive a semi alongside the tower's base. As Childs explained, the residents of Battery Park City fought the efforts to burry the West Side Highway alongside the WTC site. Had the highway been buried as part of the rebuilding effort any truck laden bomb blast would have been easily contained underground and no bomb-proofing would have been required. The problem is that that would have united Battery Park City with the rest of Manhattan, and that is not what the developers of Battery Park want.

Battery Park City is built over landfill removed from the deep foundations dug to support the original Twin Towers (the underappreciated "bathtub" that miraculously withstood the collapse of the Towers). The excavated rock and soil was dumped off the West Side Highway and it remains separated from the rest of downtown Manhattan by that wide busy roadway. Battery Park City has developed into a posh semi-private enclave. It is to New York what the Green Zone was to Baghdad: a foreign toehold, sectioned off and protected from the city around it. But instead of a fortified American exclave within a Middle Eastern war zone, Battery Park City is a Disney-esque planned community for those who work in New York, but want to live in Dallas.

Cut off by the highway, Battery Park has its own theaters, restaurants waterfront, and playfields (I have never seen anywhere else in NYC near the amount of sports equipment as on display each afternoon in BPC), all of which are so difficult for most New Yorkers to visit, that it may as well be in Dallas (it looks and feels a bit like Dallas). It is not a walled community, but it may as well be. Had the West Side Highway been buried it would have lost its exclusivity. Its parks and theaters would have become more like other New York spaces – crowded. Its fate, should crime rise in the city, would have been to suffer the crime wave with the rest of us.

But that didn't happen. With the highway in place there is no threat of that sort of reversal. The cost to the rest of us is a disfigured Freedom Tower and a disfigure New York City. Battery Park city started out like a blister on Manhattan's toe, but has grown to be a clubfoot. But the disfigurement of the World Trade Center is the same division that is disfiguring all of America. Walled communities, private security, private jets, private schools; the wealthy are abandoning our public infrastructure, and so have nothing invested in its success.

VI: A Modest Proposal for Tiananmen Square

I propose building nine Freedom Towers on this underdeveloped site. Each tower would follow the SOM design, and have a bombproof cubic base 200' X 200' X 200' of "impenetrable concrete." The towers will then rise another 1150' and finally, sprouting from a circular support ring "similar to the Statue of Liberty's torch" will be tall radio towers for a total height of 1776'. These 9 towers would fill the entire 38 acre square, allowing only narrow grid of open space for traffic – a "win-win move for development." The duel premises, that large unbroken urban spaces are fascist marching grounds in some essentialist way and that freedom can be "represented" (rather that expressed) by bombproof architecture, and can be simultaneously tested by this proposal.

In 1989 Tiananmen Square was to the site of massive pro-democracy protests, thousands of Chinese citizens were arrested, and no one knows how many were killed. The image of a man standing by himself in front of a line of tanks electrified the world, but the whole truth is that this picture of a lone figure was only possible because of the tens of thousands of men and women who stood just outside the frame. That great gathering was possible only because the crowd had the room to stand together, in mass.

While Tiananmen Square has long been the site of state sponsored pageants it is now synonymous with spontaneous popular uprising. New York City has no such place. In 2004 office of mayor Mike Bloomberg (R) protected the RNC from the possibility of a massive protest when it ruled that Central Park's Great Lawn was unsuitable for political protest because it was feared the crowds would damage the sod. Despite the fact that the sod there has repeatedly supported massive crowds for concerts, the mayor's justification stood up in court. If New York had had a large artificially surfaced space like Tiananmen Square, the authorities would not have been able to justify, even to the friendliest court, turning down a request for a public meeting.

It would seem that a free society must protect itself from political protest by foreclosing on the possibility of mass gathering. China, as it continues to liberalize, should take a page from American urban planners. Just as American cities and universities have divided and built-in the large civic spaces that hosted political protests in the 1960s; China should avoid the embarrassment of another violent crackdown by replacing the possibility of mass dissent that Tiananmen Square presents. The 38-acre site can be easily transformed from political lightning field to a symbol of freedom surpassing the dreams of American developers. While SOM's Freedom Tower is actually the bastard child of committee compromise, unrestrained commercial interests, and a Fortress America commitment to security against all possible enemies (read: fear-mongering scare tactics), it is clad in the heaviest veneer of symbolic program. No element, no matter how patently cowardly, is lacking in symbolic importance (afraid to actually build something 1776' high? Add a really tall radio tower symbolizing freedom).

If the Chinese are to develop into a vibrant commercial society like the U.S. they need to start avoiding the possibility of direct democratic processes of accountability now. The first step can be the creation of 24 million square feet of office space and destination shopping.

First published on *Rhizome* on March 21, 2012. Available online at http://rhizome.org/editorial/2012/mar/21/image-democracy-why-i-want-build-nine-freedom-towe/.

JOHN POWERS (http://starwarsmodern.blogspot.it/) divides his practice between writing and sculpture, exploring the legacies of minimalism and its attendant ideologies through both of these avenues while focusing on the interplay between popular culture – most often in the form of Star Wars – and the avant-garde. Recent projects have been presented at Performa in New York and the NODE10 Festival in Frankfurt.

Notes

[1] David Childs, *Buildings and Fear*, 2007. Video documentation, available online at http://archleague.org/risk/?p=30. Childs is Chief Architect of SOM's Freedom Tower.

[2] Cf. Naomi Wolf, *Give Me Liberty: A Handbook for American Revolutionaries*, Simon & Schuster Trade Paperbacks, 2008.

[3] Wu Hung, *Remaking Beijing: Tiananmen Square and the Creation of a Political Space,* University Of Chicago Press, 2005, pp. 7 – 8.

[4] David Childs, *Buildings and Fear*, 2007.

[5] Quoted in Michael Fried, *Art and Objecthood: Essays and Reviews*, The University of Chicago Press, 1998, pp. 154 and 159.

[6] Anna C. Chave, "Minimalism and the Rhetoric of Power," in *Arts 64*, no. 5 (January 1990): 44-63. Available online at http://annachave.com/annachave .com/annachave_publications_files/Minimalism.pdf.

[7] Cf. Raul Fornet Betancourt, "The Ethic of Care for the Self as a Practice of Freedom. An Interview with Michel Foucault", 1984. In James William Bernauer, David M. Rasmussen, *The Final Foucault*, The MIT Press 1987, p. 18.

[8] Cf. Jerry Saltz, "Clusterfuck Aesthetics. A manic-depressive panic attack in the face of profound information overload", in *The Village Voice*, November 29, 2005. Online at www.villagevoice.com/2005-11-29/art/clusterfuck-aesthetics/.

[9] Cf. Michael Kimmelman, "Restore a Gateway to Dignity", in The New York Times, February 8, 2012. Online at www.nytimes.com/2012/02/12/arts/design/a-proposal-for-penn-station-and-madison-square-garden.html.

[10] Naomi Wolf, "Naomi Wolf: how I was arrested at Occupy Wall Street", in *The Guardian*, October 19, 2011, online at http://www.guardian.co.uk/commentisfree/cifamerica/2011/oct/19/naomi-wolf-arrest-occupy-wall-street.

[11] Italo Calvino, *Le città invisibili*, Torino 1972. *Invisible Cities*, New York, Harcourt Brace Jovanovich, 1974.

Sarah Jaffe

The Cost
to Connect

Image courtesy dangerousminds.net. Graphic by Dimitri Drujchin, original photo Guillaume Paumier

A like of my photo on Instagram, a post to Twitter when an email was languishing unanswered, a view on Spotify of what music he was listening to that day became torture, after a boy I loved broke my heart and moved out of town. We'd promised to "stay friends" but in practice that just meant that our social networks, so closely entwined, served as tiny little stabs in the heart each day. The social web is just that – a web of connections, woven through multiple sites and apps but spun out of real human relationships, sometimes stretched thin or sometimes already so but made accidentally closer through the technology. I could hide him on Facebook without having to "unfriend," and I deliberately left him on Foursquare so I'd know if he came into town unannounced. These are the ways we connect and communicate today, the ways we maintain relationships and the ways it remains hard to end them.

An article this spring in *The Atlantic* by Stephen Marche wondered "Is Facebook making us lonely?" [1] Marche theorized that hyperconnectivity, epitomized by Mark Zuckerberg's human stamp collection of a website, is actually making us less connected than ever – and he discussed it with researchers who found his thesis, ultimately, inconclusive. It turns out, of course, that the loneliness or lack thereof that one derives from the Internet is much related to how one uses it.

The metaphor for the speed of connection that Marche picks up, then leaves dangling, a giant waste of a great symbol, is a connection between stock traders on Wall Street and Chicago. He shifts topics to Facebook almost as quickly as the stocks zip between trading floors, but he misses the entire point he just subtly made – what we've actually done is get better, or at least faster, at selling things, not really connecting or communicating at all.

It's capitalism, late capitalism practiced at hyperspeed, [2] with financial transactions done by computers "far faster than humans can intervene," that is pushing the $300 million fiber-optic lines Marche references, not our desire for ever-more connection. And it's capitalism that has inspired companies like Facebook to commodify our relationships and attempt to sell them back to us. It's capitalism that leaves us lonely in the wake of so much connection, not merely the existence of the Internet.

The internet, which came to us via government funding, [3] arrived in everyday households as Communism died and what Mark Fisher calls Capitalist Realism [4] – the idea that there simply is no alternative way we might organize society – came upon us. And as this massive communication machine went from being a thing you had to pay a big company by the hour to use to being a thing you could access for free from any coffee shop (or your smartphone), business had to find new ways to charge us for the privilege of talking to one another. From America Online's chatrooms, which you were paying AOL to use, we have gone to Facebook, where you are not the consumer, but the product.

The consumer that Zuckerberg wants to attract is the company willing to pay for access to the data you give Facebook to microtarget ads at you, the small business that used to be able to message its "friends" for free but is now being charged for the privilege. As writer Melissa Gira Grant (a small irony of this piece being that she's a real-life friend of mine, and thus I am quoting her on something before you've gotten to read it) says, Facebook is "a machine for creating wealth for nerds," built on the unpaid labor of millions (and the special appeal of personal access to women), posting photos, updating their status, providing more and more information.

The strangeness that Facebook inserts into each interaction, then, is not distance or disconnection, but that ad you barely notice on the side of your screen, that inaudible sound of money, somewhere, changing hands.

One of my dearest friends lives in England; we see each other perhaps three or four times a year. Yet we talk many times a week, almost always on G-chat or through email. I met him online – we met in person not long after, but it's the constant contact of the internet that really created and cemented our friendship. When he's away from the 'net for a week's vacation, I miss his presence even though he is in fact no further away than he ever is. I am lonelier when he is not there; I am less so for knowing him.

The measurable increase in loneliness that Marche notes springs from about the same time period as the internet, but also the same time period as the decline of unions, the increase in income inequality, the end of an economic system that paid even lip service to solidarity and community, and the rise of the freelance worker, "flexibility," the home office, and the telecommute. The "societal breakdown" Marche laments sprang from the conservative lips (and policies) of England's Margaret Thatcher, who famously told us there was no such thing as society, [5] and on our side of the ocean, from Ronald Reagan. The decline of unions and the isolation of working people was a deliberate strategy for cutting costs and increasing control by a well-heeled elite that saw its income spike dramatically over the last 30 or so years. Oh, and the rise of that hyperspeed finance capital, too.

"In the face of this social disintegration," Marche writes, "we have essentially hired an army of replacement confidants, an entire class of professional carers." But while Marche seems to want personal analysis, the claiming of responsibility for our own loneliness, Mark Fisher looks at the rise of mental health problems (and the physical ailments that come along with them) and calls for a re-politicization of our struggles.

"Instead of treating it as incumbent on individuals to resolve their own psychological distress," Fisher writes, "instead, that is, of accepting the vast *privatization of stress* that has taken place over the last thirty years, we need to ask: how has it become acceptable that so many people, and especially so many young people, are ill?" If loneliness is increasing across the board, if we are forced to turn to professionals (who of course charge for their services, turning yet another interpersonal relationship into something we must pay for) to maintain our mental well-being, what is this if not a social problem?

When we see our relationships as "social capital" rather than as community-building, as tools for improving ourselves rather than as contributions to a larger society, when the basic argument for having better friends and deeper connections is that they'll improve one's own health and happiness, it's hard not to think Thatcher was right.

Solidarity, a term so often misunderstood these days, is the value of standing together in community. The best demonstration that I've seen recently was Walmart workers, out on strike, telling an executive in one voice, as he offered "to meet with you individually to address any individual concerns you may have," "We are not here individually. We are here as a group." As unions have declined and strike frequency fell off [6] (though recent big ones have captured some public attention), we have seen fewer and fewer public demonstrations of solidarity; it's not accidental that the Occupy Wall Street movement and its predecessors used social networks to organize but seized control of the narrative when they gathered large groups together in public spaces.

There's been a tendency since at least Iran's Green uprisings in 2009 to credit Facebook and Twitter as being the spark of the mass protest movements, just as there was a tendency to dub first Howard Dean and then Barack Obama the "internet candidates." The power of what Clay Shirky calls "ridiculously easy group formation" [7] online is that it lowers the cost of collective organizing; the downside to this is the rise of "clicktivism," where everyone has a petition you can sign. The extreme image called up by critics is of a solitary person sitting behind a screen, passively clicking petition links and then going back to downloading porn or watching cat videos or tending their Farmville, never getting out from behind the screen.

One of the more interesting, though hardly surprising, revelations in Marche's piece comes from Moira Burke, a grad student whose study of Facebook users found that those who use the site to communicate with one another derive more happiness from it, while those who primarily use it to peruse others' pages wind up feeling more lonely. He also cites another study, by a grad student whose name he does not bother to give us, "that showed how believing that others have strong social networks can lead to feelings of depression."

Surveillance, then, coupled with envy, or perhaps competition is the better word, is what really leads us to loneliness. Watching others interact on Facebook silently, wishing for friendships you don't have, perhaps obsessing over one particular one. It was the surveillance that drove me wild when that boy left town, the occasional "like" reminding me of his existence, the photos and updates but no real contact.

(By contrast, that same information, as Deanna Zandt [8] has noted, can allow your friendships to remain closer – a passing tweet from a friend about her sinus infection led me to send a text and make plans to see her when she's next in town.)

Surveillance is a crucial component of our age; we are always being watched. Our data is collected with or without our permission by Facebook and other companies in order to better sell to us but also to determine our voting preferences, our messages mined for keywords that might spell out a future crime to law enforcement. There's a camera at the end of my Brooklyn block. Is it surprising that we've replaced meaningful communication, all too often, with the collection of information?

The newest outrage, at press time, from Facebook is the birth of new "relationship" pages, created by the site for people who've decided to check off the "in a relationship" box and inform Facebook and the world who the lucky other party is.

It's precisely the attempt to boil your "relationship" down to a string of events and photos and mutual friends and interests that is so wrong about Facebook's Relationship pages; by doing so, it highlights exactly what the Internet can never hope to capture, that spark between two people that no dating site algorithm (or indeed, in-person matchmaker) has yet to figure out how to quantify.

Because of course Facebook isn't the first site to try to commodify your relationship. It's just that most of them are trying to sell you the possibility of a relationship, offering access to other humans chosen for you by a formula or screened by photo and list of likes and dislikes or perhaps in one case, by what you'd like to do on a date. They're trying to sell you convenience as much as love, to sell you the idea that you don't need the mess, the complication, the weird human reality of feelings and interaction, of course.

Slavoj Zizek, in *The New Left Review*, notes this contradiction: "By definition... comparing qualities of respective candidates, deciding with whom to fall in love, cannot be love. This is the reason why dating agencies are an anti-love device par excellence." [9]

Or to twist a phrase of Fisher's, describing the way his students want Nietzsche without the difficulty, the struggle of learning it – the difficulty is love. It is what you don't see on Facebook.

The most strangely intimate social media contacts, I find, are Spotify and Instagram: the one shares with your friends the music you're listening to, the other your photographs of your daily life. Knowing that my friend is listening to a certain sad song on repeat brings me a more direct awareness of his mood than any status update. And I limit Instagram follows to close friends, and I'm constantly surprised when strangers want to see my endless photos of my dog, my messy bedroom, my new glasses. They're the ones that get the closest to that ineffable something between words, that spark that it's hard to describe in words.

They are also the far ends of the commodification problem, at once the easiest and the hardest to package and sell. While Spotify is a paid music service that aims to lead me to buying albums, Instagram seemed for a while to be impossible to monetize. This week, however, the internet exploded with the revelation that Instagram had changed its terms of service, perhaps making it easier for your private photos to be used in ads – without permission or compensation. [10]

In explaining what the changes actually mean (and how they are and are not an expansion of the rights the company already claimed to have to sell your life), Nilay Patel at *The Verge* wrote:

"...[T]he company will be using our personal emotional moments in a limited commercial way, even if they have no connection to the product being sold. And make no mistake: Instagram screwed up royally by publishing these new terms of service and not explaining them in any way." [11]

Patel continued, "Instagram has our photos – the company has a responsibility to tell us exactly how it plans to make money with them, even if the plans are fairly benign."

And yet, those photos are harder to quantify and to sell than a Facebook post about the new hot Hollywood blockbuster. Personal relationships are deep and meaningful only to a handful of people; they don't really increase the selling power to a broader audience very much.

This perhaps epitomizes Web 2.0, the social Internet: it both is and is not a venue for capitalism, a way to sell and be sold and also a way to connect and create and by doing so confounds those who want to boil everything down to the bottom line.

First published on *Rhizome* on December 20, 2012. Available online at http://rhizome.org/editorial/2012/dec/20/instagame/

SARAH JAFFE is a writer, a rabblerouser and frequent Twitterer. You can follow her at @sarahljaffe.

Notes

[1] Stephen Marche, "Is Facebook Making Us Lonely?", in *The Atlantic*, May 2012, online at www.theatlantic.com/magazine/archive/2012/05/is-facebook-making-us-lonely/308930/.

[2] Cf. Jerry Adler, "Raging Bulls: How Wall Street Got Addicted to Light-Speed Trading", in *Wired,* August 3, 2012, online at http://www.wired.com/business/2012/08/ff_wallstreet_trading/all/.

[3] Cf. Gregory Ferenstein, "'Father of The Internet', Vint Cerf, Says Government Gets Credit For Inventing Web", in *Tech Crunch,* July 26, 2012, online at http://techcrunch.com/2012/07/26/father-of-the-internet-vint-cerf-says-government-gets-credit-for-inventing-web/.

[4] Cf. Matthew Fuller, "Questioning Capitalist Realism: An Interview with Mark Fisher", in *MR Zine*, December 27, 2009, online at http://mrzine.monthlyreview.org/2009/fisher271209.html.

[5] Cf. Peter Beresford, "From 'no such thing as society' to 'big society'. Spot the difference", in *The Guardian*, July 11, 2011. Online at http://www.guardian.co.uk/society/joepublic/2011/jul/11/big-society-no-such-thing-as-society.

[6] Doug Henwood, "Strike wave!", August 8, 2010, in *LBO News*, online at http://lbo-news.com/2010/08/18/strike-wave/.

[7] Cf. [Internet & Democracy Blog], "Clay Shirky on Organizing Without Organizations", February 28, 2008, online at https://blogs.law.harvard.edu/idblog/2008/02/28/clay-shirky-on-organizing-without-organizations/.

[8] Cf. Amanda Marcotte, "FDL Book Salon Welcomes Deanna Zandt, Share This!", June 27, 2010, online at http://firedoglake.com/2010/06/27/fdl-book-salon-welcomes-deanna-zandt-share-this/.

[9] In Slavoj Žižek, "A Permanent Economic Emergency", in *New Left Review 64*, July-August 2010. Online at http://newleftreview.org/II/64/slavoj-zizek-a-permanent-economic-emergency.

[10] Instagram ultimately chose to retract those changes: cf. Chris Welch, "PSA: Instagram's new (and old) terms of service go into effect today", in *The Verge*, January 19, 2013, online at www.theverge.com/2013/1/19/3892924/instagram-new-tos-go-into-effect-today.

[11] Nilay Patel, "No, Instagram can't sell your photos: what the new terms of service really mean", in *The Verge*, December 18, 2012. Online at www.theverge.com/2012/12/18/3780158/instagrams-new-terms-of-service-what-they-really-mean.

Harry Burke

Love
Letters

Anafi. Image courtesy The Eternal Internet Brotherhood

The following essay first appeared on the website for The Eternal Internet Brotherhood, a gathering of artists, writers, curators and others interested in internet culture on the greek island of Anafi from August 9th until the 23rd. It was written by Burke while attending the event.

love letter

I've decided to write love letters because that's what you do when you're in love. I saw that great document today – all text and in a block, from Slovenia, I think. It was from the 90s. So basically, people got together, and they found an old or cheap building, and they inserted a sound system or bands or DJs, and for 36hrs or more they would dance, presumably, make out, get together, find myriad tangents through the throbbing artery of night. And by morning they couldn't even see each other, just feel under their shoes the concrete, every little pore of it. They'd sleep in the cracks for half an hour, and get up and go again, right back where they started, that firstness again. And that amazing 90s hair, just enough gel still in for that cow's lip, or curtains, throbbing, clothes that were all sportswear and primary colours. Showing the bottom part of your fist to each other, and pumping it. Chewing your own lips. Smiles that contorted and scarred our faces. Imagine finding someone in that moment, every freeze frame of the artificial lighting their body getting closer, each a different angle, a different record sleeve. And they don't even look up, you just know as the record needle moves inwards that there's an ultimate trajectory to all of this, you call it in your molten state a teleology, and in the repetitive stuttering beat on which all life is you hear, every revolution, "Hegel". Or maybe that's just the noise in the cracks in the ceiling, or maybe it's some sort of broken signal, maybe it's the sound the lights make. You think you hear it behind you, and you turn round, and then she's dancing with you. All this is anachronistic of course. All these famous spaces are closed down, unopen, all the ravers with jobs and even family. Seagulls flying round them, broken bottles nesting by fences, all the detritus of late Communism, late Capitalism, everything. They go there still though, to this day, maybe once in their whole adult lifetime, just to walk round, slightly underdressed in the consistent maritime wind, thinking that was me once, that was a different me, I can see the ghost of me floating through the floor, those quiet revolutions, on repeat. Or was it everytime a different me? That was the one time it was ever the same me, and I left it there. Or something like that, melancholia, whatever. No one ever thinks, imagine dancing there now. Imagine that moment where you just say, let's go back to mine. And being there not even talking when you know the whole thing is still going on, Hegel Hegel Hegel, the music melting through you. Just lying there, our heads touching.

How can this be love? This is love that's a small ontological simplicity. Like knowing there's music playing. And around that, is all of us. I'm sitting by the motorway, on the balcony. I'm sitting watching the motorway moan. And how it snakes off violently, forever. As if Ulysses comes stuttering back, shirt off, on his scooter. Imagine, his chest armored with hair, him smelling of brandy, wearing those tight red shorts and speedo swimming pool sandals. Hey baby I love you. Hegel Hegel Hegel. Writing about love is the most selfish thing in the world. This heat here is unbearable. 42 degrees. Too hot even for the Akropolis. I wonder am I writing love; am I literally trying to write love, is writing violent? The motorway right to the mouth of the river. Ulysses wearing aftershave.

love letter

In the circle where we sit I look at you. We never catch eyes, but I study the edge of your cheeks, the relationship between your eyes and their freckles, the abyss of your shirt collar. I think of nothing in this moment, but elsewhere around me there are sculptors in their studios carving statues for money, hammering on in the Classical tradition. It's ok though, right, my grandmother had one. Right by the carpet by the electric fireplace. We played lego. We often talk about sex. And I wonder: is it possible to have sex without penetration? Can we have sex without actually having sex? Is it socially acceptable for us to surround each other, it imbue each other, to add colour to each other, but that be all. Guilt for loving you. My guilt reflex for loving. My father depends on my mother. And I remember how empowered I felt when I told someone that my father can't actually write, and they didn't really understand it, and I only just in that moment realized. He can't actually write, like when you write the alphabet. Thank god for computers. And typewriters. Together we talk about sex. So anyway, I was thinking last night, although this might just have been my standing on an Athenian beach in 30+ degree heat: I might have an idea of a contribution for my Embodiment day. So, it would be very low-key, and might probably just consist of an announcement at the beginning. The announcement would be: "This will not be in any way enforced, and I won't ever remind you or check up on this at any point again, but I'd like to encourage that we kiss each other on the lips as a convivial greeting, or a goodbye. Or at least, I'm just wondering if we could accept it as socially ok amongst each other, between us as friends, and maybe not see it as wrong or weird, and therefore ok if people do it. Depends on what you feel comfortable with. Maybe it will seem the right thing to do at the end of the day, maybe totally the opposite. I'm not sure, but I've just been thinking recently, imagine if everyone did it, and it was just normal." Ok end of announcement, and we all just move on, but the thought's there, and the intervention's been made, I think. Do you think that will make people feel really uncomfortable? Or excited? Maybe both. Why? This is just want one of those things that I totally don't understand, and that makes me curious to think more about it. Maybe it's just something we'll start doing in Anafi. When no one even realises it is the best bit. We say hello to each other and kiss, because that's what I would have wanted to happen anyway. There's this recurring fantasy of mine: the city, surrounding us, embalming us, rearranging itself around us. When you're stood in the middle of the road and your phone goes off, and you don't even have to answer it to know. Us hanging out at Centre Point, knowing we're on top of each other. They make high-rises because they know this, they sit on top of the city and surround it. We serve them canapés. But really it's us that surrounds them. They can't leave their penthouse, because it no longer exists, and all around them capital is collapsing, and people are demonstrating, cheering, hating capital. And that moment is when it happens, capital's collapsing and we don't even know what is is, we're in the eye of it all, fucking. Recurring fantasy: my saying I love you. You say nothing but you know.

love letter

Acknowledging the patriarchy. Ok so we know. Ok let's talk about the male hegemony over the world. Don't chastise me for writing about this, the point is we're invisible and should be everywhere, right. We take responsibility for what we do. And how to address this if we're scared. Talking to a Quebecois about this on a Greek path, hazy Ouzo reality, smash the patriarchy. Us two males walking down a Greek path talking about the patriarchy, drunk. The internal irony. Smash the patriarchy. Future action now. Walking down the path and getting to the bottom, obviously. And there I had love, and couldn't even talk about it. We're in control of our own abstract power dynamics, and guess what they're not abstract. And maybe we're not male at all, we're just told we are by the other males, all fragments of the big abiding male. We wish we were. And then all the males have sex. Who would you want to have in the room right now to talk about this? Who would you like to confront? I read the Metahaven [1] book today, and antagonism is at the heart of us and them. Antagonism is at the heart of difference. The patriarchy wants flatness, because flatness is what they're used to: twitter, facebook, the internet: flatness. The horizontal is a hierarchy. Organic foods for everyone, right. The dude abides. Nowhere else but Greece, and the gays with all their chests out, and my lazy, wandering eyes. Eye fucking because you couldn't do it in the industrial era. My latent suppressed homosexuality. The party at the top of the hill tonight. Capitalism reduced to just describing things. Crisis. I wish you were here. I wish you were here and you are. Sleeping next to you, occasionally kissing you, wishing I could speak more to you. It's really absurd, us sleeping together and I've been reading *Ulysses* recently and all I had in my head in the morning was Blaze-boiling Blazes Boylan, looping and repeating. And as that recurred, I got ever more dehydrated, dirty, dry. Language spinning around us, and all these letters just to tell you that we slept together. The point is that I can't speak to you directly. Our world is a catalogue of window frames, it's you outside mine. The point is that we built the frame together. Lol imagine love poems in 2020. I want to fly with you on Concorde. I think this was originally a group discussion, but I'm not sure how to initiate things here, apart from in secret ways, hands touching in the sand. Instead let's paint each other's bodies, and be together in the future. It's exhausting here; I'll sleep with you.

love letter

Alex Ross's *Eltham Open* opens tomorrow at Gerald Moore Gallery, all the way past Brockley. It's open for one day, and it features Julia Tcharfas, Samara Scott et al designing mini golf holes. These are then played by the viewer / participant. All this is part of their Summer School, which is art and education in August. I write about this because I couldn't avoid it on facebook. Obviously I've come to Greece to get away from it all – pure escapism – but still. I can't help but want to keep up. A friend's event, attended by friends, being advertised by yet more friends. Hashtag fomo. I guess i would have gone if I could. I think these letters are the place to say the most suppressed, most obvious things. Him sitting there in his leather jacket, amazing. I never did send him my dissertation. He never emailed me. But the *Eltham Open* is interesting in its own way. Allan Kaprow, the father of the

Happening, described in 1958 the Participatory Event as, "A game, an adventure, a number of activities engaged in by participants for the sake of playing." [2] The *Eltham Open*, when taken in these terms, is undoubtedly a Happening. It is openly and ephemerally Participatory Art, long after it ceased to be cool. It is perfectly, quirkily, Hayward: if this was once art on the 'outside', it is now, quite unabashedly, the suburbs, replete with its own cafe. Yet if the original Happenings developed in historicity with '60s Participatory Politics, and in opposition to what we later recognise as 'Spectacle', Alex's evolution of it seems complicit with a more insidious and lurid reality. My point being: how can we read Kaprow's words as anything but the mechanics and metrics of gamification? The '60s seem so quaint and beatnik-ish today, all their anger so misdirected and irrelevant. There's no longer such thing as the Society of the Spectacle. But instead there's something much worse, something more everpresent and pernicious. Maybe we call it the Society of the Social, maybe we even give it capital letters. It's no longer the image that's the breeding ground of capital, but the way we share, interact with, and even befriend these images. It's the process of interaction itself. The thing that happens when we have internet in the town square by the school by where they filmed the man playing bagpipes is find each other on facebook. I tell everyone I hate facebook, still around us we're on facebook. And right now I'm telling my friends about it. Game over. Gamify insurrection. Cycling by the river, not even allowed to cross the footbridge, winning the game of rock / paper / scissors. I was taking part in a cycling protest, and wasn't allowed to cross north of the river, even on my own, and I lied about it and they made me play rock / paper / scissors so I could go home to my home in Manor House which conveniently I didn't have any documentation proving anything about, and I won. And then so frustrated for a week, drinking alcohol and talking about it, hating it, and then of course now writing these love letters. Vincent said a really good thing: the spectacle made relational. Of course Alex knows this, and this is the secret beauty of it all. How can we escape this double bind? Hard to say, but not by not playing it. And in a facebook that's breaking down, post by post and image by image collapsing in on itself, its ubiquity, I can't even access how the event was shared.

love letter

I'm so privileged because I know most people won't even look at these, they really won't care, that's the point of calling them love letters. This one's purely for you, everyone else can stop reading now: stop reading. Imagine writing letters for other emotions. Distrust letter: I fundamentally distrust you, just like I distrust alt-lit. Ultimately, everyone else will be repulsed by love letters. Maybe that's part of it too – it's total rejection otherwise. Chris Kraus loves dick? Everyone on this island is naked, Angelo [3] says. Everyone here should be naked. On the nudist beach. Nudism implies considered rejection of civilisation. It is one of the clearest forms of body-as-context. You wear no clothes because you know that surrounding you are laws that, were they written, would be 9000 years old, maybe more. It is the ability to disconnect that shows we are connected. And so the Greek man who walks down the beach nude and goes for a swim carries every Hewlett-Packard processor in every provincial business park across the world. It is society that surrounds him, that makes him fully clothed. Our body is a network of occurrences; the boat we arrived on, the tent we sleep in, the plane that connects me to you: all this is part of our body. And so I glow when you touch me. Imagine Gilles Deleuze sitting here, making African pyres on the beach. Around him, all of us, is a primitivist ceremony. Afterwards we go the taverna for dinner. Their ashes, that's where I hide you.

In their shadow, we'll connect each other, because that's what we're told to do. When we fuck each other, that's when we know we have bodies. Our body is a network of occurrences. Can we change it? Are we trapped? What are we trapped in? The present order was founded on desire. Desire is the death moment, is where we die. I think I decided to write love letters because of their some spatio-temporal peculiarity. As in, these are desires trapped in a peculiar and small fold; disconnected and fully, eternally, nonlinear. They are memories that I blemish in recording them, send outwards, anywhere, and disown. At the same time you pick them up, at whatever small juncture of your life, and they have material impact on you, on your life. You might even see imminently after, but I'll have disowned them, attempting to impose linearity on the context that surrounds me called normal. We'll know therefore that it's a missed connection, a small slippage, but also a shared territory. Does that make them any less or more real? They're still a shared territory, a more beautifully latent slippage. Being on holiday feels like this, storing up possible returns, future ignition to any number of the looping and multilinear contexts with which we clothe ourselves. And after all this, anyway, I'm still sat on the nudist beach, wondering how to have sex, wanting to swim round the corner and have sex on the secret beach there, like an otter glistening in the sand, wanting to talk about sex and have sex by just talking. Foucault said something like this, we should always analyse our present moment, because these are the invisible power structures that create us. He also said that recognition of power is just as significant a development as the recognition of slavery, but it might take just as long to understand and abolish. His students trailing him as he walked into the sex shop. My falling asleep straight away, my secret wholeness, my embarrassment, our perfection. Imagine seeing each other and not even talking about this.

First published on *Rhizome* on August 20, 2012. Available online at
http://rhizome.org/editorial/2012/aug/20/love-letters/

HARRY BURKE (http://harryburke.tv) is a writer and curator based in London. He has written for *Rhizome*, *Arcadia Missa Publications* and *Fulcrum*, a publication based at the Architectural Association, and curated the exhibition *Net Narrative* at Carlos/Ishikawa. His poems can be found here: http://harryburke.tv/junkspace.html.

Notes

[1] Metahaven (Daniel van der Velden, Vinca Kruk) with Marina Vishmidt, *Uncorporate Identity*, Lars Müller Publishers, Amsterdam 2010.
[2] Cf. Dick Higgins, "The Origin of Happening," *American Speech*, Vol. 51, No. 3/4 (Autumn - Winter, 1976): 268.
[3] Angelo Plessas, artist, founder of the Angelo Foundation and organizer of the Eternal Internet Brotherhood.

126

Giampaolo Bianconi

Gifability

A frame from an anonymous animated GIF inspired by Annie (Alison Brie) running down the hallway in part 1 of "Community's" season finale, "A Fistful of Paintballs."

Last winter, Dan Harmon, who was then the executive producer of the television sitcom *Community,* shared that he tried, "many times a season" to put star Alison Brie "in a situation, wardrobe-wise, that I know is going to end up as an animated GIF file!" [1] Those GIFs, which circulate on Tumblr and other social media networks that traffic in images, are frame-capture GIFs. Unlike other GIF types, frame-capture GIFs plainly collect and endlessly repeat a single pop cultural moment from movies, TV shows, sporting events, political occasions, newscasts, cartoons, or even video games. As GIFs are silent, text is used to share dialogue or help shepherd the meaning of a GIF. Frame-grab GIFs are low-quality, incessantly mobile things, they can be awkwardly cropped and their focus is always obviously legible. Somewhat counter to this are what Daniel Rourke has termed art GIFs, [2] which, while also frequently sourced from movies or television, contain higher resolutions and have highbrow pretension, usually focusing on subtler, "artistic" moments. Writing in the early 1990s, Susan

Stewart observed that

"with the advent of film, interpretation has been replaced by watching… Here we see the increasing historical tendency toward the self-sufficient machine, the sign that generates all consequent signs, the Frankenstein and the thinking computer that have the capacity to erase their authors and, even more significantly, to erase the labor of their authors." [3]

Stewart's diagnosis of the filmic watching-state returns, in a modified form, with the frame-grab GIF. These GIFs are in some sense the ultimate in self-sufficiency, not merely in the eternal return of their endless loop, but also within what Rourke has called the co-ordination of "their own realm of correspondence." [4]

The quality of the frame-grab GIF is important. Borrowing insights from Hito Steyerl's analysis of the poor image, the creation and distribution of frame-grab GIFs "enables the user's active participation in the creation and distribution of content, it also drafts them into production. Users become editors, critics, translators, and (co)authors of poor images." [5] Perhaps due to their quality and size, frame-grab GIFs have necessarily abstracted authorship. They are deployed in variable contexts, as reactions, illustrations, or expressions. Art GIFs, on the other hand, are circulated to be admired. Their authorship is also more consistently policed, as their authors demand credit for their work.

While Stewart's description of "the sign that generates all consequent signs" is one that erases authorship, the vernacular of frame-grab GIFs does something different. Instead of completely erasing authorship, the creation of frame-grab GIFs rearranges its tenets. Generally centered on a performer, framing the actor / actress in a context removed from the narrative flow of their source media. With their behavior on display, they carry a kind of performative authorial focus within the GIF. While the GIF is not by them, it is of them.

While GIFs may originate as souvenirs of viewership, they quickly begin to perform a different function. As Steyerl emphasizes, the labor of the frame-grab GIF comes from a place of postproduction. Stewart's watching paradigm is further revised by the level of interactivity and manipulation that emerges as an extension of traditional spectatorship. Capturing, regurgitating, looping, and distributing become regularized postproduction activities. "Collective postproduction," Steyerl has written, "Generates not only composite bodies but composite works." [6] As GIFs engage in their own mobility, they begin to articulate in different ways.

The potential of GIFability is already expected by producers of media, like Dan Harmon, who see it as a way to appease their audiences. Because in a sense, no work is complete until it has been GIFed. The GIF allows for an almost seamless level of pure circulation, especially the frame-grab GIF, which is so small as to be negligible. And if something can become a platform for a GIF, it can become a platform for its own movement, metonymically, across the Internet. This sentiment holds within it the hope that despite the decontextualization of the frame-grab GIF, it will retain at least a trace of its origin. More so, it is a hope that they carry their context with them, and become badges of pop culture connoisseurship for people looking to share their tastes.

Producers may hope that post-producers will create GIFs that, when seen, will encourage them to seek out the surrounding media. Given the fragment, one will wish to complete it. When fragmented into a frame-grab GIF, is what remains a piece of a puzzle – an incomplete remainder that needs to fit back into its linear narrative – or is it a new, seditious totality? The fragment, as understood within Romanticism, is experienced like a ruin: an irreconcilable trace of pastness within the modern world. Like the ruin, the origin of the fragment is unattainable: to be understood, it must be recontextualized.

The creation of a new totality within the GIF ensures its dexterity throughout variable recontextualizations: the many ways in which the contingency of fragmentary meaning and context are tested as GIFs are used as responses, expressions, and illustrations. Their existence as a fragment doesn't serve as a preamble to the restoration of the whole: it perpetuates a continuation of the fragmentary, as emphasized by its endless looping, its pure existence for its own moment without a need to desire to belong to another stream of narrative. As Steyerl has articulated, the supplement of postproduction overtakes its object: "Post-production has begun to take over production wholesale." [7] With the dispersion of the frame-grab GIF, the fragmentation surpasses its place of origin. The frame-grab GIF becomes the locus of meaning, the creation of an Internet vernacular utilizing our visual literacy.

Language carries the weight of idioms derived from once-routine activities. GIFs form an idiomatic language rooted in a communal experience not of labor or action but spectatorship and postproduction. "An ocean of viral videos turned into a self-serving visual language, looping back on itself ad-infinitum." [8] The degrees of our literacy expand as well: we create GIFs combining GIFs, and they circulate and articulate as well.

Describing a contemporary iteration of Paul Klee's *Angelus Novus* "inflated and replicated on a giant balloon inside an artificial entertainment world," [9] Steyerl observes that this *Angelus Novus* has no forward movement:

*"It looks down on a paradise without sin and without history, in which the future has been replaced by the promise of temporary upward mobility. **The horizon loops**. An angel becomes drone; divine violence divested into killing time." [10]*

Instead of the detritus of history, this angel witnesses an already decided state of historicity. The looping horizon could be a future deprived of history, but this perpetual looping as a property of the GIF indicates something else. The creation and collision of GIFs offers a potentially different implication for the looping horizon: the possibility of communication. Benjamin cast Klee's *Angelus Novus* as a witness to the debris, or fragments, of history. A divine being, what for us constitutes history is to him only the perpetual accumulation of wreckage. Despite the destruction – and the angel's desire to "make whole what has been smashed" [11] – he is propelled ceaselessly forward by a violent storm. Now, perhaps trapped before a looping horizon, we promote an inverted relationship of understanding: presented with supposedly whole media artifacts, we deconstruct and disperse them, wreck them and from the rubble construct a new lexicon of associations and meanings.

First published on *Rhizome* on November 20, 2012. Available online at http://rhizome.org/editorial/2012/nov/20/gifability/

GIAMPAOLO BIANCONI is a regular contributor to *Rhizome*. His writing has also appeared in *Idiom*, *The Brooklyn Rail*, and *Modern Matter*. He lives in Brooklyn.

Notes

[1] Cf. Morgan Jeffery, "'Community' Dan Harmon Q&A: 'Our fans influence the show'", in Digital Spy, November 9, 2011. Online at www.digitalspy.com/tv/interviews/a349824/community-dan-harmon-qa-our-fans-influence-the-show.html.

[2] Daniel Rourke, "The Doctrine of the Similar (GIF GIF GIF)", May 25, 2011, online at http://machinemachine.net/text/ideas/the-doctrine-of-the-similar-GIF-GIF-GIF.

[3] Susan Stewart, *On Longing: Narratives of the Miniature, the Gigantic, the Souvenir, the Collection*, Durham: Duke University Press, 1996 (1993). 11.

[4] Rourke 2011.

[5] Hito Steyerl, "In Defense of the Poor Image", in *e-flux journal*, Issue 10, November 2009, online at www.e-flux.com/journal/in-defense-of-the-poor-image/.

[6] Hito Steyerl, "Cut! Reproduction and Recombination", in *The Wretched of the Screen*, Sternberg Press, New York 2012. 176-190. 187.

[7] Ibid. 182.

[8] Rourke 2011.

[9] Steyerl 2012: 185. Emphasis mine.

[10] Ibid. 186. Divine violence divested into killing time, I think, has two meanings: one of course that the Benjaminian notion of divine violence has been displaced into the perpetual awareness and murderous potential of the drone. Second, though, there is a sense in which people, perpetually postproducing, become drones just "killing time."

[11] Walter Benjamin, "Theses on the Philosophy of History", in *Illuminations*, New York: Schlocken Books, 2007. 253-264. 257.

Jason Huff

Beyond the Surface: 15 Years of Desktop Aesthetics

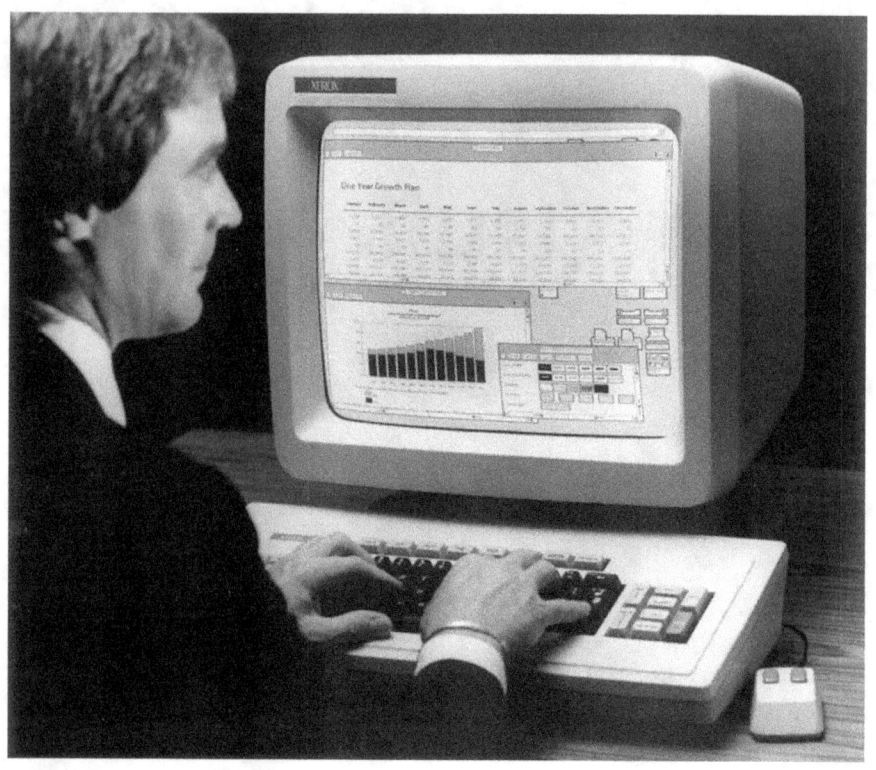

The Xerox Star 8010 Workstation (1981) – Image via plyojump.com

A desktop is a changing record of visual decisions. It speaks to the aesthetics of a particular work-flow and personal space. A desktop exhibits a diagram of your organizational habits and a screenshot of it captures a brief moment of its functional evolution. The image of your desktop becomes an intimate self-portrait and the impulse to decode an unfamiliar desktop is unavoidable.

In January, artist Adam Cruces wrapped up his *Desktop Views* [1] project. Cruces collected 51 images of artists' desktops including a number of artists he worked with in his earlier project STATE. [2]

Cruces frames *Desktop Views* with a quote from Alexei Shulgin's legendary *Desktop Is* [3] project, created 15 years earlier in 1997, at the dawn of "net.art." The quote, taken from the about page of Shulgin's project, uses the title *Desktop Is* as an iterative I Ching-style manifesto about the desktop. Its final lines claim in paradox, "desktop is a question, desktop is the answer." Cruces's description of *Desktop Views* is more straightforward and less poetic. To him the desktop is "the (virtual) space that serves as the foundation of the working environment." Cruces and Shulgin, however, channel the same curiosity. The two projects are echoes that present voyeuristic peeks into artists' personal virtual working spaces on public websites.

The *Desktop Is* site is a deteriorated time capsule. Its nostalgic Apple OS desktop interface links to two folders; one, leads to site information, and the second, to a list of submitted desktop images. Link rot has broken nearly half of the links in Shulgin's list of submissions and the ones that work are a mix of cryptic handles, like Murph the surf, in contrast to full names – some followed by an email address.

In converse, Cruces's new iteration, *Desktop Views* is standardized. It presents a grid of images (a sort of meta desktop) that can be sorted alphabetically by first name or chronologically in the order they were collected and released on the site. Artists' full names label each desktop thumbnail in the grid. Cruces hosts all the images he has collected, so perhaps this archive of desktop images will remain intact for more complete future reflections. Within the order, the desktop images range from stark defaults to extreme clutter.

Sara Ludy's desktop, for example, is minimal with a blurred blue smudge of pixels centered on a black background. On the right side, vased.mov is immediately above vased.gif which might reveal a recently created animated gif. Daniel Keller's desktop image presents a more complex space. His numerous file icons stand in an equally spaced array – small and unreadable. They vanish into an endless crowded background of solar panels stacked edge-to-edge.

Martin Murphy's desktop has a strange background image: a hand wrapped in latex touches a warped smiling face in a pool of purple color. The face stares out of the screen. Icons, floating on the right, are grid-free and vaguely organized. Three external drive mounts show a potential need for more space while a folder announces a "project with Evan" in its name. Perhaps this counts as evidence of collaboration. Amidst bluetooth connections, a dropbox account, and a desirable suite of creative software applications in the dock below, Murphy is present. He listens to Spotify and captured his desktop image with OS X's Grab application.

Some visual clues reveal location or language, like Jon Rafman's Canadian flag in his menu bar. His background image shows two men climbing a floating knot of infinite stairs up and down, down and up. A handgun icon labelled "TODO" floats point-blank at one man's head. Other desktops are more mysterious. Rafael Rozendaal's blank grey background leaves everything to the imagination – his tiny system activity monitor, maxed out in red and green, is the only leading detail.

While Cruces's project feels curatorial, Shulgin's is more ethnographic. When Shulgin started *Desktop Is* in October of 1997 he sent an email out to a mailing list and proposed to accept submissions for six months. It is impossible to determine if everyone who submitted was an artist, but Shulgin had started the "net.art" mailing list approximately two-months before which might help classify the list of linked names.

Seen as a broader survey the desktop images of *Desktop Is* accomplish two things: They historicize the nostalgic aesthetics of

90s desktops and help frame newer artists working with technology in a longer view. With each iterative software and hardware update, however, we wash bits of that history away.

So what can we learn by reconsidering desktop aesthetics 15 years later? The default structure and icons of operating systems are more or less the same. They have not changed substantially since Xerox designed Star, a pioneer in graphic user interfaces in 1981, which was refined slightly by Apple in 1983. The biggest difference is in the color space. The pixelated palette moved from binary black and white, to the 16 colors of early versions of Windows, graduating finally to modern operating systems which are anti-aliased and millions of colors deep. Clunky and outdated window, button, and menu graphics have all been refined – smoothed, over a long period of time, like river stones.

Icons offer the most concrete evidence of what has survived and what is new. The core icon set of operating systems still clings to skeumorphs that help us relate abstracted digital data forms to their ancestors. The physical file folder, for example, was introduced at the invention of the filing cabinet in 1898 and remains the inspiration for the default folder icon. Even on the earliest desktop, a document was represented by a single sheet of paper with the top right corner folded at a comical 45 degree angle. Thirty years later that folded corner has a subtle shadow, gradient, and tradition.

Photoshop's icon has survived the decade or more of upgrades too. Its transformation spans from its original monochrome, pixel-edged eye-in-window to the new, dark, sans serif "PS" pressed softly with a shadow into an extruded blue gradient block.

Older desktop images in Shulgin's *Desktop Is* collection feel arcane and nostalgic – pixelated microfilm. At the time, it was the eve of the dot-com bubble, and Windows and Netscape Navigator were commonplace. Screenshots in *Desktop Is* have grit in both content and color depth. Some, like Rachel Baker's, contain coded political phrases in the folder names while other desktops mock the virtual space's infinite potential. Fast-forward 15 years – Windows is no longer a common OS for artists, and Netscape Navigator is extinct. Artists use OS X and Google Chrome. The new desktop images from artists are hi-res, smooth, or ironically pixelated.

But the curiosity of private desktop space shown publicly withstands software and hardware upgrades. Interpretations of layout, background image, icon size, and other details that describe a human presence – or lack of one – hold weight. The question is not about aesthetics, but about how artists create and use their desktop space.

To answer this, *The Guardian* started a series [4] profiling writers and their desktops. It takes a dual approach: a desktop image with a parallel explanation. The series begins with Ben Johncock interviewing Tom McCarthy [5] about his submitted desktop image, which captures a few open folders in addition to the typical background image and icon grid. The open folders reveal deeper personal information as McCarthy takes us through a few of the folder names that relate to projects he is working on. This is all mixed in with conversation about technology's affect on his writing and on humanity at large. The desktop becomes a room for conversation about work and leisure, and a platform for reflection and speculation on technology.

When I asked Cruces over email to describe his own desktop image on the about page of *Desktop Views* he replied:

"I think it's quite reflective of how I utilize my physical spaces (apartment and studio). I prefer to keep things tidy and organized – concealing personal items, tools, materials, works in progress, and final products."

Desktops are the new studio. In the 1930s people were captivated by photographs of Francis Bacon's London studio – a dark cluttered mess of half-used paint tubes, gnarled brushes, and stained walls. Now we can look at these desktop images with the same memorializing curiosity – all the while trying to decode who created them.

First published on *Rhizome* on March 14, 2012. Available online at http://rhizome.org/editorial/2012/mar/14/beyond-surface-15-years-desktop-aesthetics/.

JASON HUFF (http://www.jason-huff.com/) is a New York-based conceptual artist investigating the intersection of internet culture and the everyday. His work has been exhibited internationally and is included in the Special Collections at the Whitney Museum of American Art. He is a contributor at *Rhizome*, *Artinfo*, and *Modern Painters*.

Notes

[1] Cf. http://desktop-views.com/.
[2] Cf.http://thestate.tumblr.com/.
[3] Cf. http://www.easylife.org/desktop/.
[4] Available online at www.guardian.co.uk/books/series/writers-desktops.
[5] Ben Johncock, "Tom McCarthy: My desktop", in *The Guardian*, November 24, 2011, online at www.guardian.co.uk/books/2011/nov/24/tom-mccarthy-desktop.

Clement Valla

The Universal Texture

143

Clement Valla, *The Universal Texture*, 2012. Inkjet on Canvas, 44 inches x 92 inches each. Courtesy the artist

"These artists [...] counter the database, understood as a structure of dehumanized power, with the collection, as a form of idiosyncratic, unsystematic, and human memory. They collect what interests them, whatever they feel can and should be included in a meaning system. They describe, critique, and finally challenge the dynamics of the database, forcing it to evolve." [1]

I collect Google Earth images. I discovered them by accident, these particularly strange snapshots, where the illusion of a seamless and accurate representation of the Earth's surface seems to break down. I was Google Earth-ing, when I noticed that a striking number of buildings looked like they were upside down. I could tell there were two competing visual inputs here – the 3D model that formed the surface of the earth, and the mapping of the aerial photography; they didn't match up. Depth cues in the aerial photographs, like shadows and lighting, were not aligning with the depth cues of the 3D model.

The competing visual inputs I had noticed produced some exceptional imagery, and I began to find more and start a collection. At first, I thought they were glitches, or errors in the algorithm, but looking closer, I realized the situation was actually more interesting – these images are not glitches. They are the absolute logical result of the system. They are an edge condition – an anomaly within the system, a nonstandard, an outlier, even, but not an error. These jarring moments expose how Google Earth works, focusing our attention on the software. They are seams which reveal a new model of seeing and of representing our world – as dynamic, ever-changing data from a myriad of different sources – endlessly combined, constantly updated, creating a seamless illusion.

3D Images like those in Google Earth are generated through a process called texture mapping. Texture mapping is a technology developed by Ed Catmull in the 1970's. In 3D modeling, a texture map is a flat image that gets applied to the surface of a 3D model, like a label on a can or a bottle of soda. Textures typically represent a flat expanse with very little depth of field, meant to mimic surface properties of an object. Textures are more like a scan than a photograph. The surface represented in a texture coincides with the surface of the picture plane, unlike a photograph that represents a space beyond the picture plane. This difference might be summed up another way: we see through a photograph, we look at a texture. This is an important distinction in 3D modeling, because textures are stretched across the surface of a 3D model, in essence becoming the skin for the model.

Google Earth's textures however, are not shallow or flat. They are photographs that we look through into a space represented beyond – a space our brain interprets as having three dimensions and depth. We see space in the aerial photographs because of light and shadows and because of our prior knowledge of experienced space. When these photographs get distorted and stretched across the 3D topography of the earth, we are both looking at the distorted picture plane, and through the same picture plane at the space depicted in the texture. In other words, we are looking at two spaces simultaneously. Most of the time this doubling of spaces in Google Earth goes unnoticed, but sometimes the two spaces are so different, that things look strange, vertiginous, or plain wrong. But they're not wrong. They reveal Google's system used to map the earth – The Universal Texture.

The Universal Texture is a Google patent for mapping textures onto a 3D model of the entire globe. [2] At its core the Universal Texture is just an optimal way to generate a texture map of the earth. As its name implies, the Universal Texture promises a god-like (or drone-like) uninterrupted navigation of our planet – not a tiled series of discrete maps, but a flowing and fluid experience. This experience is so different, so much more seamless than previous technologies, that it is an achievement quite like what the escalator did to shopping:

"No invention has had the importance for and impact on shopping as the escalator. As opposed to the elevator, which is limited in terms of the numbers it can transport between different floors and which through its very mechanism insists on division, the escalator accommodates and combines any flow, efficiently creates fluid transitions between one level and another, and even blurs the distinction between separate levels and individual spaces." [3]

In the digital media world, this fluid continuity is analogous to the infinite scroll's effect on Tumblr. In Google Earth, the Universal Texture delivers a smooth, complete and easily accessible knowledge of the planet's surface. The Universal Texture is able to take a giant photo collage made up of aerial photographs from all kinds of different sources – various companies, governments, mapping institutes – and map it onto a three-dimensional model assembled from as many distinct sources. It blends these disparate data together into a seamless space – like the escalator merges floors in a shopping mall.

Our mechanical processes for creating images have habituated us into thinking in terms of snapshots – discrete segments of time and space (no matter how close together those discrete segments get, we still count in frames per second and image aspect ratios). But Google is thinking in continuity. The images produced by Google Earth are quite unlike a photograph that bears an indexical relationship to a given space at a given time. Rather, they are hybrid images, a patchwork of two-dimensional photographic data and three-dimensional topographic data extracted from a slew of sources, data-mined, pre-processed, blended and merged in real-time. Google Earth is essentially a database disguised as a photographic representation.

It is an automated, statistical, incessant, universal representation that selectively chooses its data. (For one, there is no 'night' in Google's version of Earth.) The system edits a particular representation of the world. The software edits, re-assembles, processes and packages reality in order to form a very specific and useful model. These collected images feel alien, because they are clearly an incorrect representation of the earth's surface. And it is precisely because humans did not directly create these images that they are so fascinating. They are created by an algorithm that finds nothing wrong in these moments. They are less a creation, than a kind of fact – a representation of the laws of the Universal Texture. As a collection the anomalies are a weird natural history of Google Earth's software. They are strange new typologies, representative of a particular digital process. Typically, the illusion the Universal Texture creates makes the process itself go unnoticed, but these anomalies offer a glimpse into the data collection and assembly. They bring the diverging data sources to light. In these anomalies we understand there are competing inputs, competing data sources and discrepancy in the data. The world is not so fluid after all.

By capturing screenshots of these images in Google Earth, I am pausing them and pulling them out of the update cycle. I capture these images to archive them – to make sure there is a record that this image was produced by the Universal Texture at a particular time and place. As I kept looking for more anomalies, and revisiting anomalies I had already discovered, I noticed the images I had discovered were disappearing. The aerial photographs were getting updated, becoming 'flatter' – from being taken at less of an angle or having the shadows below bridges muted. Because Google Earth is constantly updating its algorithms and three-dimensional data, each specific moment could only be captured as a still image. I know Google is trying to fix some of these anomalies too – I've been contacted by a Google engineer who has come up with a clever fix for the problem of drooping roads and bridges. Though the change has yet to appear in the software, it's only a matter of time.

Taking a closer look, Google's algorithms also seem to have a way to select certain types of aerial photographs over others, so as more photographs are taken, the better ones get selected. To Google, better photographs are flatter, have fewer shadows and are taken from higher angles. Because of this progress, these strange images are being erased. I see part of my work as archiving these temporal digital typologies. I also call these images postcards to cast myself as a tourist in the temporal and virtual space – a space that exists digitally for a moment, and may perhaps never be reconstituted again by any computer.

Nothing draws more attention to the temporality of these images than the simple observation that the clouds are disappearing from Google Earth. After all, clouds obscures the surface of the planet so photos with no clouds are privileged. The Universal Texture and its attendant database algorithms are trained on a few basic qualitative traits – no clouds, high contrast, shallow depth, daylight photos. Progress in architecture has given us total control over interior environments; climate controlled spaces smoothly connected by escalators in shopping malls, airports, hotels and casinos. Progress in the Universal Texture promises to give us a smooth and continuous 24-hour, cloudless, daylit world, increasingly free of jarring anomalies, outliers and statistical inconsistency.

First published on *Rhizome* on July 31, 2012. Available online at http://rhizome.org/editorial/2012/jul/31/universal-texture/.

CLEMENT VALLA (http://clementvalla.com/) began using computers and digital technologies to explore formal, mathematical, linguistic and social systems. He is interested in processes that produce unfamiliar artifacts and skew reality. Clement works within systems, applying a 'programmed brain' that pushes problem-solving logic to irrational ends.

Notes:

[1] Domenico Quaranta, "Collect the WWWorld. The Artist as Archivist in the Internet Age," in Domenico Quaranta et al., *Collect the WWWorld*, exhibition catalogue, LINK Editions, September 2011.
[2] For more information, check out chapter 2 of the "WebGL Earth Documentation", available online at http://data.webglearth.com/doc/.
[3] Srdjan Jovanovic Weiss, Sze Tsung Leong, "Escalator," in Koolhaas et al., *Harvard Design School Guide to Shopping*, Köln, New York, Taschen, 2001.

Rachel Wetzler

The Art of Fieldwork

Simon Fujiwara, *The Personal Effects of Theo Grünberg*, 2010. Mixed media installation and performance. Photo credit: Anders Sune Berg. Image courtesy Kunsthal Charlottenborg.

In 2008, the New York-based artist Ellie Ga joined the crew of the Tara, a sailboat drifting in the Arctic Ocean as part of a scientific expedition, occupying the incongruous position of the ship's "artist-in-residence" among a team of scientific researchers. The role of "artist in residence" on a scientific expedition is a malleable one, without clearly defined parameters, thus Ga decided that her project would be to become the ship's archivist, attempting to capture the various facets of life aboard the Tara: the ways in which the crew organized the world around them without conventional landmarks; how they entertained themselves; the sense of uncertainty that results from following the whims of weather patterns, never quite knowing where they would move next; as well as her own personal associations and insights about the expedition and their surroundings, unburdened by the demands of scientific fact or reportage.

In the resulting body of work, which has taken various forms, including lectures, performances, slideshows, and videos, her personal narratives and memories often occupy a central role. In the performance *Reading the Deck of Tara* at the Lower East Side gallery Bureau in 2011, visitors were given one-on-one readings with the artist herself, in which she used a custom deck of cards inspired by those used in fortunetelling to relay aspects of her life aboard Tara. Each visitor's particular cards determined the form and content of the narrative, with each reading – and thus each version of the story she'd tell – being particular to that visitor, the performance's element of chance echoing the movement of a ship adrift.

Borrowing methods from various disciplines, from sociology to fiction writing, Ga is one of a number of younger contemporary artists whose work is tied to a kind of artistic fieldwork, investigating aspects of their lives and interests by merging the apparent objectivity of documentary forms and anthropological research with a plainly subjective, flexible approach, drawing on multiple methodologies and discourses. While the "archival impulse" [1] in contemporary art is hardly a new phenomenon, and research-oriented practices have arguably become the norm rather than the exception, what seems to differentiate work like Ga's from those that fall under the broad, often contested banner of "relational," "dialogical," or "socially-engaged art," is that the endgame here isn't to offer a historiographic corrective or engage an outside community; rather, the role of artist is treated as license to borrow freely, to temporarily adopt and explore different modes of working, living, or thinking.

Like Ga, New York-based Swedish artist Sara Jordenö's projects also often take the form of atypical archives, presenting the results of her research in the form of films, installations, animations, drawings, and text. Heavily informed by sociology, she has referred to her work as "performative investigations," highlighting the tensions implicit in artistic research and the shifting roles she plays in the process of creating it. *The Persona Project* (2000-2010) is a work in seven parts revolving around Ingmar Bergman's 1966 film *Persona*, the artist's favorite film. Created over the course of a decade, the resulting archive examines what Jordenö describes as the film's "peripheral" voices: those impacting the film's creation, circulation, and reception but rarely, if ever, considered, ranging from translators and voice-over actors to the woman who lives in the house where Persona was filmed. Ultimately the archive Jordenö creates with *The Persona Project* is an idiosyncratic one, less a portrait of Bergman's *Persona* – its ostensible subject – than a reflection of the artist's own concerns mediated through a form of near-obsessive research.

Similarly, her project *Diamond People – Instructions for a Film* (2010) examines issues of labor and globalization through an investigation into the synthetic diamond industry in Sweden, South Africa, and China. However, the project goes beyond merely charting the relationship between these geographically distant and yet economically intertwined sites. Combining more typically "documentary" media like photography and video with drawing, poetry, and animation, the project equally reflects Jordenö's concern with the implications of her anthropological approach and her own shifting relationship to the subjects of her inquiry. One of the places she considers is her hometown, the Swedish industrial town of Robertsfors, whose synthetic diamond factory was her first employer. The subtitle, "Instructions for a film," is itself enigmatic, hinting at something in need of assembly, as in industrial manufacturing, but also suggesting a work-in-progress, or perhaps even a coy invitation to the viewer to take up the task of attempting to resolve the project's inherent complexities and contradictions.

Though his projects might appear, at first glance, to have little in common with Jordenö's, the Berlin-based British artist Simon Fujiwara is similarly concerned with adopting multiple roles to probe aspects of his own personal history, casting himself variously as anthropologist, architect, novelist, and raconteur. In the project *The Museum of Incest* (2008), Fujiwara created a proposal for a museum at the "Cradle of Mankind" in Africa, where many of the oldest hominid fossils have been discovered. The premise for Fujiwara's museum is that the origins of man are rooted in incest, envisioning an alternative natural history museum in which we are all products of society's greatest taboo. Drawing on the conventions of academic lectures and archaeological displays, the absurd proposal includes an exploration of the architectural complex that would house the museum, composed of parts of existing buildings designed by Fujiwara's architect father.

Likewise, for the multi-layered project *Welcome to The Hotel Munber* (2010), the artist took inspiration from a hotel owned and operated by his parents in Franco's Spain during the 1970s, reconstructing the hotel bar based on descriptions and photographs, and attempting to write an erotic novel set in it, casting his father as the gay protagonist. When presenting the work as a lecture, Fujiwara similarly adopts a pseudo-academic mode, combining extracts from his fictionalized narrative of his parents' life in Spain with their photographs, memorabilia from the hotel, and newspaper clippings, blurring the boundaries between the factual and fictional. That a dramatized version of *Welcome to the Hotel Mumber* formed the second act of Fujiwara's recent Performa commission *The Boy Who Cried Wolf* (2012) only serves to further challenge our ability to distinguish between the elements Fujiwara has invented wholesale and those that are accurate recollections of events.

When asked, in a 2009 interview, about the ways in which he adopts various identities in creating his works, borrowing from their tropes and methodologies, but never fully conforming to their professional standards, Fujiwara responded:

Who says I'm not a writer or an architect or anything? Who has the authority to decide these things? [...] Honestly, I am a fraud, I'm an outsider in all these fields, but this gives me the liberty to work subjectively. Truth and accuracy are not my concerns. If an academic would work with fiction in this way, it would be dishonest, wrong even, whereas you'd be a fool to trust an artist in the first place. [2]

Fujiwara's quote might arguably best sum up this tendency: if art can be anything, then the artist can also be anyone. Though their work is strikingly different in process and final form, Ga, Jordenö, and Fujiwara, to consider only a few of the artists working in this vein, explore the possibilities offered by different disciplines, choosing to be as rigorous – or as lax – as they see fit. Yet, rather than resulting in watered-down versions of social science, in which the methods of a more supposedly "serious" field are employed to confer a veneer of relevance or gravity on an artistic project, the work of these artists is enlivened by the marrying of the subjective and idiosyncratic with the academic and research-intensive.

For a younger generation of artists, for whom the use of technology is natural and the Internet an inextricable part of information gathering, the ability to adopt these various strategies and roles is greatly enhanced by the accessibility of information: in an Internet age, the barriers to research begin to collapse. While these projects are typically presented in a physical format – as an installation, a book, a film, a performance, and so on – what is striking is that the form itself is flexible; the artists discussed here have presented the results of their research in multiple ways, allowing each project to take on several different incarnations.

This, too, arguably reflects a new attitude towards a research-based practice, and the influence of the digital world: rather than conceiving of their work as a physical entity, with a particular, fixed form, it is instead versatile and open-ended.

First published on *Rhizome* on February 2, 2012. Available online at http://rhizome.org/editorial/2012/feb/2/artist-ethnographer/.

RACHEL WETZLER (http://rachelwetzler.com/) is a New York-based critic and a doctoral student in Art History at CUNY Graduate Center.

Notes

[1] The expression is borrowed from Hal Foster, "An Archival Impulse", in *October 110*, Fall 2004: 3-22.
[2] Francesca Boenzi, "Sexual Architecture. Simon Fujiwara", in *Mousse Magazine*, Issue 20, 2009. Online at www.moussemagazine.it/articolo.mm?id=460.

Yin Ho

Shu Lea Cheang on Brandon

Shu Lea Cheang, *Brandon: Bigdoll interface*, 1998. Collaboration with Jordy Jones and Cherise Fong. Image courtesy the artist

In 1998, the Guggenheim Museum launched its first web-based art commission, Shu Lea Cheang's Brandon. Over the course of a year, the collaborative, dynamic piece would look at the complexity of gender, sexuality, and identity through the life and death of Brandon Teena / Teena Brandon, a Nebraska youth who was raped and murdered after his biological sex as a woman came to light in 1993.

Oft-cited in new media art history as one of the first widely recognized pieces of net art, the Brandon site has been offline for the last year or so; the Guggenheim plans to restore the work in the very near future.

Cheang now resides and works in Paris. I spoke to her about Brandon, 14 years after its launch.

YH: How did you first come to conceptualize *Brandon*? What were the circumstances for its commission?

SLC: Brandon was conceived at a time that I moved from actual space to cyber / virtual, claiming myself a cyber-nomad. It was around the mid-90s, and there was high hope for a super-highway, for a virtual world where race / gender does not matter any more. (I think it was the ad copy of MCI communications?). Meanwhile, two articles came out at *Village Voice*, one about Brandon Teena's rape / murder case by Donna Minkowitz [1] and the other Julian Dibbell's *A Rape in Cyberspace*. [2] I had been experimenting with boundary crossing between the actual (state / nation) and virtual (anonymous / avatars), which needed to take up a durational performative format.

By 1995, I wrote out a proposal which was to be a one-year web narrative project following my feature film *Fresh Kill* (1994). At the time, I guess it was unusual to conceive a durational web work, to be unfolded by episodes, by staged virtual performance 'events' supported by actual space installation. At the time, David Ross was the director of the Whitney Museum. He had the vision to expand the museum into cyberspace. Curator John Hanhardt – who has exhibited three of my major works: *color schemes* (a solo show in 1990), *Those Fluttering Objects of Desire* (1993, Whitney Biennial), and *Fresh Kill* (1995, Whitney Biennial) – took up the curation of *Brandon*. By 1998, Hanhardt had moved to the Guggenheim Museum and took *Brandon* with him. At the Guggenheim, Matthew Drutt, Associate Curator for Research, helped realize the curatorial amidst the Guggenheim's venture into the virtual museum with Asymptote Architects.

YH: How were you thinking of interfaces? Did your work in film and other medium inform how you work in digital form?

SLC: The interfaces in *Brandon* – bigdoll, roadtrip, mooplay, panopticon, and Theatrum Anatomicum – are each a launch pad, a collaborative platform. Each interface is programmed as a mainframe, a structural construct while the contents and the inhabitants can move in and out in flux. While the programming language is definitive, the narrative shifts and progresses with more add-ons and plug-ins.

Yes, I do come from a video installation and film production background. In films, my narrative is parallel, non-linear. In installations, I also have multi-streams narratives proposed by the collaborators. I leapt into netspace (digital is a recent term), bypassing the CD-ROM format, where I see the streams converge with open circuit possibilities.

YH: Materially, did you have to consider the technology platforms on which *Brandon* would be run? Where did the images that appear onsite come from (were they all culled from the internet / of digital or physical origin)?

SLC: Yes. Surely. Please also remember *Brandon* is a multi-artist, multi-site, multi-institution collaboration. Each interface is a design / programming with others, mostly working with, i.e. Javascript and Java applet. Today, many of these programming languages have been updated, i.e., AV streaming. Many images are works by various designers (i.e., Jordy Jones, Auriea Harvey). There were also actual court documents from the Brandon Teena trial.

YH: There are several interfaces and the architecture of the site itself is discoverable by interaction. I had the sense that I was finding fragments of an identity. What were you thinking when you created those interactions, different interfaces, and pop-up windows? Was the piece

envisioned primarily as web-based? How did you modify the piece for the video wall installation? Did any of your conceptual tenets adjust for its physical mode?

SLC: Brandon is like a puzzle? I guess. It was deliberately designed with no easy / clear marked icons to help you navigate through the site. One's ability to investigate, negotiate with the mouse(over) brings different experience of the work. Within a one year stretch, which includes installation, live chat format, actual / virtual performance, no one (including myself) can claim to have viewed the entirety of this work. Pop-up windows on the roadtrip interface, cells of panopticon interface, are alien expansion of the space, spaces to be occupied by various narratives and inhabitants. Surely, non-linear and non-conformative.

Yes, the work was conceived for the web space. However, there remains the necessity at the time to have a real space for public interaction. The exhibition at the Guggenheim Soho's multi-screenwall is a direct translation of the website with kiosks for mouse interaction. I was also able to create installations that 'bridge' actual / virtual with the Theatrum Anatomicum installations set up at Waag Society in Amsterdam from 1998 to 1999. The opportunity to work with the Institute on Arts and Civic Dialogue in collaboration with Harvard Law School allowed for the realization [3] of actual / virtual court rooms scenes in "Would the Jurors Please Stand Up? Crime and Punishment as Net Spectacle." I guess I would have done it if there were no real space offered. But with the real spaces, they offer great chances to merge the actual / virtual public.

YH: What was the response to the piece when it appeared? When did it go offline and were there specific reasons it went offline? How does not being able to see a piece impact its existence?

SLC: There was great enthusiasm about this work, for its grand scale, its unprecedented approach to web art. It has been used a lot by media art students and there were several Ph.D. dissertations based on this work.

The Brandon website started out with a sponsored server which was terminated. Then, it was moved to an in-house Guggenheim server managed by its IT department. Around 2005, there was a great reconstruction effort with some funds for digital preservation. It was also brought back in two media art exhibitions, one with Rhizome at the New Museum and the other in *The Art Formerly Known As New Media* at Banff Canada. In this past year, the website was offline (I don't know for what reason, exactly) and created much confusion for media art studies – I constantly received complaints about it.

Recently, there are efforts to restore this work online by the Guggenheim's collection and curatorial departments. A rather long story, indeed.

First published on *Rhizome* on May 10, 2012. Online at
http://rhizome.org/editorial/2012/may/10/shu-lea-cheang-on-brandon/.

YIN HO is an artist and contributing writer at *Rhizome*.

Notes

[1] Donna Minkowitz, "Love Hurts", in *The Village Voice*, April 19, 1994. Online at www.villagevoice.com/2005-10-18/specials/culture-clash/7/.
[2] Julian Dibbell, "A Rape in Cyberspace", in *The Village Voice*, December 23, 1993, online at www.juliandibbell.com/texts/bungle_vv.html.
[3] Cf. Beverly Hanly, "Body of Evidence", in *Wired*, August 5, 1998, online at www.wired.com/culture/lifestyle/news/1998/08/14219.

Ben Fino-Radin

When Machines Speak

The VODER on show at the New Museum, New York, for the exhibition *Ghosts in the Machine*. Courtesy New Museum, New York. Photo: Benoit Pailley

In July of 2012, The New Museum of Contemporary Art staged the exhibition *Ghosts in the Machine*. [1] Curated by Massimiliano Gioni and Gary Carrion-Murayari, the exhibition was "conceived as an encyclopedic cabinet of wonders: bringing together an array of artworks and non-art objects to create an unsystematic archive of man's attempt to reconcile the organic and the mechanical." [2] Of the myriad works presented in the exhibition, there was one humble object that in so many ways embodies the complex history of technical abstraction, and the externalization of that which is inherently human. This object is called the VODER.

Short for Voice Operation DEmonstratoR, the VODER was an instrument or tool that provided its operator the ability to synthesize human speech. It easily predates the first cases of computerized speech synthesis, and represents the distinct end of an era for a particular type of metonymic device, along with the beginning of a whole other era of synthesized speech. The year was 1929. As the story goes, Bell Labs researcher Homer Dudley experienced an epiphanic moment, while laying in a hospital bed.

A pioneering researcher of voice communications technologies, Dudley was working to develop more efficient methods of voice transmission that could make better use of the Bell System's bandwidth. His eureka moment was the realization that the human mechanisms of speech (the vocal cords, mouth, teeth, tongue and lips), resembled the mechanics of radio transmission: [3] the vocal chords create high-frequency vibrations that serve essentially as a carrier wave to the data encoded by the articulations of the mouth. He would go on to spearhead the development of technology that enabled the invention of a device called the Vocoder. [4] By breaking speech down into ten low frequency bands, the Vocoder was able to send transmissions requiring far less bandwidth than the full spectral information produced by the telephone. By the mid-30s the team at Bell Labs had developed these technologies to successful ends, but would not see implementation outside of the lab for another decade or so.

It was this initial work on the Vocoder that led Dudley down a winding path toward the VODER. The key distinction between the Vocoder and VODER is that while the Vocoder was a tool through which to process speech, the VODER was a instrument with which one could synthesize speech. The Vocoder required its operator to only turn a few knobs, and speak into a microphone. The VODER was an instrument in a wholly other sense, providing fourteen keys, a bar controlled by the operator's wrist, and a foot pedal. The Voder was not spoken to – it was performed, or played. The operator's speech impulses would bypass their destination of the vocal cords and mouth, instead manifesting themselves through their hands, wrist and foot, and finally through the manipulation of the VODER's controls. Complex combinations of keys would produce the requisite components of speech that a given letter, word, and sentence is composed of. The foot pedal controlled pitch, providing the essential subtle variations of intonation. The resultant sounds approached that of modern speech synthesis. Computers would not meet the expressive abilities of the VODER for another twenty years.

"…in producing the word 'concentration' on the VODER, I have to form thirteen different sounds in succession, make five up and down movements of the wrist bar, and vary the position of the foot pedal three to five times, according to what expression I want the VODER to give the word, and of course all this must be done with exactly correct timing." [5]

The history embedded in the VODER is truly a crossroads. It represents a moment in time where we were learning what machines sounded like when they spoke. The VODER certainly has precedence, with inventions such as the Euphonia (1835, Joseph Faber). The Euphonia was in many ways similar to the VODER in that it was a human operated instrument that attempted to reproduce the sounds of human speech. Due however to the culture in which the Euphonia was deployed, its reception was one of horror at best. The apparatus produced speech that was inexpressive and raspy – closer to a death rattle – and emanated from a prosthetic face. Pre-dating the public debut of Bell's telephone by forty one years, the Euphonia (much like the telephone) was perceived as inhuman, soulless, and downright creepy. [6] Nearly a century later, with a world accustomed to disembodied speech, it is unsurprising that a speaking machine would receive a warmer welcome.

The moment of the VODER's debut at the 1939 World's Fair can not be overstated in its significance. Here was the modern world hearing the voice of the machine for the first time. Prior to this point, any portrayal of speaking machines, automatons, robots, were pure speculation with scant evidence as an aural basis. Incredibly, Flushing Meadows-Corona Park paid witness to the collision, or passing of these two moments of pre-synthetic speech and post-synthetic speech. The Westinghouse company held a demonstration of their ELEKTRO robot. A hulking, hardly functional novelty act, this automaton carried on a conversation with great wit, and even enjoyed a cigarette on stage. There was no VODER / ELEKTRO collaboration, and with the exhibition predating formant speech synthesis [7] by over ten years, it comes as no surprise that the voice of this machine was merely a man with a microphone, speaking awkwardly (a charade with precedence tracing back to ancient Greece [8]). This strongly highlights the metonymic crossroads embodied by the VODER. Were ELEKTRO to have debuted post-VODER, it is arguable that it would have been voiced differently.

Once the true voice of the machine had entered the public consciousness, it's place and form in fictional portrayal would never be the same. After that day in 1939, we knew specifically how inhuman machined speech should sound. As the years pass beyond 1939, and we see advancements in speech synthesis, eventually leading to the first speaking computers. As technologies bring realities into being, they dictate the boundaries of what must be imagined. By 1961 the first speaking and singing computer, the IBM 704 has emerged. The circuitry that afforded the IBM machine to sing was a form of Vocoder technology.

While in decades prior, the mere notion of a seemingly sentient computer would be sufficiently disturbing, this boundary too needed renegotiation. It follows naturally, that in 1968 when crafting the cadence of HAL, Kubrick came to the decision that flawless, impeccable speech was a more stirring possibility than the stiff sounding computers of the day. It is no coincidence either, that HAL sings the same song that was first sung by the IBM 704, as Arthur C. Clarke witnessed the machine performing the song while visiting Bell Labs in 1962. [9]

The VODER truly ushered in the golden age of speech synthesis, and expanded the imagination of an era, yet it never lived to see any practical use. What exactly drove Homer Dudley to develop it? Perhaps it is best seen as an artifact representative of a perspective in contrast to the critique, caution, and even paranoia of technology embodied by some of the works in *Ghosts in the Machine*. It represents exploration for mere innovation – the curiosity of what may lie beyond the boundary of our current reality. It represents a desire to speak to our inventions, and the hope that they might talk back.

First published on *Rhizome* on August 8, 2012. Available online at http://rhizome.org/editorial/2012/aug/8/when-machines-speak/.

BEN FINO-RADIN is a New York based media archeologist, and conservator of born-digital or computer based works of contemporary art. At Rhizome, he leads the preservation and curation of the ArtBase, one of the oldest and most comprehensive collections of born-digital works of art. He is also in practice in the conservation department of the Museum of Modern Art, managing the development of a digital conservation repository, and contributing to born-digital conservation initiatives.

Notes

[1] "Ghosts in the Machine", The New Museum, New York, July 18 - September 30, 2012. Curated by Massimiliano Gioni and Gary Carrion-Murayari.

[2] Cf. www.newmuseum.org/exhibitions/view/ghosts-in-the-machine.

[3] Fully articulated eleven years later in *The Bell System Technical Journal*, Volume 19, No. 4, 1940, pp. 495, online at www.alcatel-lucent.com/bstj/vol19-1940/articles/bstj19-4-495.pdf.

[4] In his book *How to Wreck a Nice Beach,* author Dave Tompkins fully extrapolates the history of the Vocoder, tracking its evolution from cryptographic speech transmission, to its implementation in musical instruments, and subsequent adoption by generations of musicians. Cf. Dave Tompkins, *How to Wreck a Nice Beach. The Vocoder from World War II to Hip-Hop*, Stop Smiling Books, Chicago / Melville House Publishing, Brooklyn 2010.

[5] Excerpt from VODER demonstration, available online at http://ptolemy.eecs.berkeley.edu/~eal/audio/voder.wav.

[6] Cf. "Euphonia Speaking Machine", in *Dead Media Archive*, online at http://cultureandcommunication.org/deadmedia/index.php/Euphonia_Speaking_Machine.

[7] Cf. *Wikipedia*, http://en.wikipedia.org/wiki/Speech_synthesis.

[8] Thomas L. Hankins, Robert J. Silverman, "Vox Mechanica: The History of the Speaking Machine", in *Instruments and the Imagination*, Princeton University Press, 1995: 178-220.

[9] Cf. www.bell-labs.com/news/1997/march/5/2.html.

Paul Graham Raven

This Is A Game: Nordic Larp

Equinox, March 2007. Photo by danielleblue (www.flickr.com/photos/danielleblue/)

Another World Is Possible

"Larp can change the world."

So claimed Heikki Holmås, Norway's newly-appointed Minister for International Development back in March, [1] and I couldn't help but take notice. Three months previous, I was out researching an article on the Collapsonomics movement [2] when the conversation turned to the new direction in which larp players from the Nordic nations were taking the form.

Larp – which you may have encountered already as LARP, acronym of "live action roleplaying", now noun'd down into lower case by regular use – has been around long enough for its public image to settle into an established stereotype, namely nerds dressing up as knights and orcs and hitting each other with rubber swords at the weekend. Like all clichés, it's rooted in truth: a lot of larp is exactly like that – and as such, I'd argue, no more worthy of mockery than paintballing, its over-macho cousin.

But there was, I heard, another type of larp: a larp whose potential as a tool for political and social change inspired Holmås to evangelise about it; a larp that could not only give players an insight into the lived experience of, for instance, homelessness, refugeeism or gender disparity, but which might also suggest changes to the way society deals with people in those situations; a larp that could 'game out' better ways of responding to a Haiti-scale natural disaster, or help the two sides of an interminable religiopolitical stalemate to walk a few yards in the shoes of their opponents.

I scribbled some notes, went home and started digging.

A (Very) Brief History of Larp

Larp's roots run deeper than Dungeons & Dragons.

In her book *Leaving Mundania*, [3] Lizzie Stark traces the development of larp from its origins, the nascent form of what Bruce Sterling likes to call the military-entertainment complex: immersive historical pageants thrown by medieval royalty, often at immense expense; prototypical wargames for training the officers of the European enlightenment; contemporary historical re-enactment groups, some simply restaging the great battles of the past, or – in the case of the Society for Creative Anachronism – doing what they call 'living history', where old skills and ways of life are revived as part performance, part play, all wrapped up in authentic period costumes.

Wargaming systems of a more realist (or at least mimetic) type were a popular pastime for well-to-do Victorian folk, but it took a man named Dave Wesley form Minneapolis-St. Paul, frustrated with the way that the wargames he played in would break down into arguments over the implementation of the rules, to investigate the theory of games with an aim to developing non-zero-sum scenarios. The first run of *Braunstein*, a Napoleonic battle rendered with miniature soldiers on a tabletop landscape, ended in intrigue and chaos, with Wesley feeling he'd failed. "His players disagreed, and begged him to run another session," says Stark, so he did.

Braunstein attracted others, including one Dave Arneson, who'd go on to combine his wargaming jones with his *Lord Of The Rings* obsession to build a new set of rules, developed in collaboration with a thirty-something insurance underwriter named Gary Gygax; the first edition of *Dungeons & Dragons*, the ur-RPG, hit shelves in 1974.

Leaving the Tabletop

Larp was less born than seeded, however. Says Stark,

"there is no single 'mother larp' that started the craze; instead it rose up like some grassroots political campaign, with people in different areas of the United States and elsewhere spontaneously deciding to hit their friends with padded sticks in backyards." [4]

There's a possible Patient Zero in the imaginary planet of Atzor, an early proto-larp described in a *Life* article in 1941 which at the time of writing boasted ten 'lands' or countries wherein conflicts were decided with tabletop wargames of vast and involving complexity. But it's Brian Wiese's *Hobbit War* of 1977 that represents the likely apotheosis of 'boffer' larp, familiar from the pop-cultural stereotype: Ren Fair rejects, running around in the woods with padded weapons.

Tolkienian secondary-world fantasy is no longer the only aesthetic in town, however: dystopian near-futures (with varying levels of cyberpunkiness pumped into the main mix), slipstreamish alternate histories and Moorcockian multiverses also abound.

The degree of determinism to the gameplay varies wildly, as do the player goals: from get-the-loot-and-kill-the-baddies to more abstract or intangible accomplishments, such as acquiring secret knowledge or building a network of spies. This movement away from both the tabletop and the rubber weapon was amplified by the huge popularity of White Wolf Publishing's *Vampire: The Masquerade* roleplaying system and its expansions, which stripped tabletop play down to raw simplicity while (re)introducing the critters-of-the-night tropes which now dominate the nebulous 'urban fantasy' fiction genre, and may well have played a large part in priming its audience. (The White Wolf gameworld was also an early staging ground for another of network culture's oddest performative / theatrical subcultures, the furries, who found in it a safe space to explore their supposed 'species dysphoria'.)

Modern larps might be played in person in the interstitial corridors of a gaming or sci-fi convention, or online via bulletin boards and forums, or both. Games may be mere hours long, or even shorter, like the bite-sized quarter-hour 'roleplaying poems'; some games may persist for years.

What they hold in common is their escapist intent: larp is supposed to be fun, a holiday from more mundane concerns, entertainment.

It's just a game.

This is Also a Game: Nordic Larp

"Many Nordic larps seem to be about trying out a certain mindset or exploring an emotion, rather than saving a town from orcs or finding enough loot to buy a sweet magic item." - Lizzie Stark [5]

Some time close to the culture-warping strange attractor of the Millennium, however, larp underwent a development fork.

The first Knutepunkt [6] conference of 1997, held in Oslo, was an early step in the formation of the Nordic larp identity. As the conference hopped from nation to Nordic nation on a yearly basis (each time relocalising its name into the language of the host country), it brought together game designers and players interested in transcending mere entertainment, in raising larp to the level of art.

First played in 1998, *Ground Zero* has a good claim to ur-game status, and is a great example of the 'un-fun' ideas that Nordic larp plays with: its players sat in a room standing in for an Ohio nuclear shelter circa the Cuban Missile Crisis, listening to mocked-up radio reports of a blossoming bout of Mutually Assured Destruction, then spent the rest of the game having their characters come to terms with the annihilation of the world outside. Far from being an outlier, the deep emotional implications of *Ground Zero* are indicative of the psychological spaces that Nordic larp would go on to explore.

For the sake of simplicity, I'll be following Stark's lead and using 'Nordic larp' to refer specifically to the avant-garde school of gameplay rather than the geographically-defined set of players. As Stark is careful to point out, larp in the Nordic countries is not a monolith so much as a collection of localised scenes, and the Knudepunkt circuit – despite its greater visibility to outsiders – is a marginal part of the greater whole.

Marginal it may be, but Nordic larp is a teeming ecosystem of styles and approaches which, again, mirrors the confusion of subgenres and styles to be found in the contemporary genre fiction scene.

For instance, medieval-esque fantasy isn't completely off the menu. Paralleling the recent rehabilitation of epic fantasy fiction, some Nordic scenesters are returning to the massively-multiplayer orcs-in-the-woods format with historio-mythical accuracy on their minds: *Täällä Kirjokannen alla* sought to give Tolkienian cliché the boot, and provide all the rompy fun of a trad boffer game with an authentic backdrop based on Finnish mythology. Indeed, the examination of national identity seems to be a popular project for Nordic larp as it spreads southward into Europe; in Poland, a game called *Dzikie Pola* [7] began in the early Noughties, overlaying the lives of its players with an alternate reality in which they were noblemen from the Sarmatian Period.

Another obsession shared by Nordic larp with contemporary science fiction – and, not coincidentally, with pop culture in general – is the near-future or alt-history dystopia. Some of these games are huge productions, with days of gameplay following weeks of planning and set-construction; *System Danmarc*, for instance, took over a city-centre park, surrounding it with fences and filling it with shipping-container housing for the stratified underclass factions of its player-characters.

Many of these games involve a simple sort of imaginative play: one may be pretending to be another person, but that person is recognisably human, and interacts with a recognisably human imaginary world in familiar ways, despite the shifted context in which their actions take place. But not all Nordic larps bear such a clear resemblance to the mainstream forms of the game, or indeed such a mimetic resemblance to consensus reality. The Nordic methodology – which often includes a preliminary 'workshop' wherein the players are prepared for the game, perhaps with a discussion of history or politics pertinent to the larp in question, and a 'debriefing' that seeks to integrate the game experience and cushion the come-down of returning to reality – allows for set-ups and scenarios that reframe the human experience in dramatically powerful contexts.

Designed by the Nordic scene's uber-academic Emma Wieslander, *Mellan himmel och hav* ("Between Heaven and Sea", 2004) ambitiously concretised elements of feminist theory in order to explore disparity and gender roles. On joining the game, Stark explains, players were no longer male or female, but

"morning people and evening people. Evening people wore red and yellow, concerned themselves with philosophy and decision making, and served as the objects of the sexual gaze. Morning people wore blue and green, served as the sexual initiators, and were resp for practical arrangements and implementing the decisions of the evening people.
In-game, marriage was not between two people, but among four – two morning and two evening people, who mated for life." [8]

Other larps have attempted to bridge the divide with experimental and participatory theatre, or explore situations originally presented in literature – there was a larp based on de Sade's *120 Days In Sodom*, for instance. Even the mechanics of play are not sacred, with a considerable degree of experimentation into ways of abstracting character interactions which might be dangerous.

Nordic larp, then, is not easily encapsulated, though there are underlying commonalities. One thing that becomes clear early on is the doctrine of subjectivity: due to the nature of the larp experience, it is impossible to report on what a game was like from any perspective other than one's own. As such, post-game papers and reports tend to focus on design and theory rather than assessments of success or failure, or attempts to reproduce the narrative on the page; as Dave Wesley discovered with the earliest runs of *Braunstein*, a game might be a complete flop in the eyes of its designers while the players are having the time of their lives.

This was the experience of the gamewrights behind *Valokaari*, a near-future war scenario; they failed to engineer the expectations of the players – failed to assert the genre and tropes of the game before it began, if you like – and lost control of the narrative as they'd planned it. The players had a blast, however, and with the breezy insight that seems typical to Nordic gamewrights, this was viewed as a valuable lesson rather than a waste of time:

"[E]nvision you are running an *Ally McBeal* larp and then realize your players have chosen to play it like *Law & Order*. The subject matter of 'law' remains, but emphasis is very different". [9]

Games Without Frontiers

It seems to me that almost all artforms undergo a developmental curve which starts in pure entertainment and / or escapism before arching upward (or downward, depending on one's position relative to the axes) as the canon, loaming beneath its own accreted density, becomes an ecosystem able to support theorists, metacritical practices and experimental methodologies.

A similar curve is reiterated in microcosm within art genres: witness, for example, the slow development of science fiction from pulpy romps for Competent Men to its current status, that of a genre with its own canon, critical vocabulary and – perhaps most importantly – its own vanguards of theory and praxis.

It is important to note, however, that the pulpy end of the genre has not only survived but remained largely dominant in terms of sales, and also indirectly supports the avant-garde by providing an economic base for the industry: as regrettable as the posthumous eking out of Robert Jordan's bloated *Wheel Of Time* [10] series may seem to those of us who have read widely enough to recognise it as derivative, its gangbuster sales figures allow Tor to continue taking chances on new or lesser-known writers, some of whom may be pushing the form to new places.

Although that economic connection doesn't pertain (or so I assume), the development of 'literary' and avant-garde praxis and theory within science fiction and fantasy provides a useful analogy for the development of Nordic larp.

The academics, artists and players of the Nordic scene refer to more generic games as 'mainstream' larp, reserving the 'Nordic' soubriquet for their own experiments with the form. Implicit here is the claim that their Nordic larp is capital-letter Art, while the other stuff – as Capote is alleged to have said of Kerouac's work – is "just typing".

(One might compare and contrast this reframing with science fiction's snooty dismissal of mimetic fiction as 'mainstream' or 'mundane'... and, indeed, with the science fiction avant-garde's dismissal of the popular mass of push-button tropes and cliches which lurks beneath the bell-curve as 'skiffy' or 'pulp'.)

Pulp vs. Lit

"The Nordic scene is proof that fun is not a necessary or essential component of larp, proof that the hobby can sustain high-art aspirations." - Lizzie Stark [11]

In the course of her investigations, Stark has played a variety of larps, from big-business Stateside boffers like *Knight Realms* to mind-bending art-school Nordic oddities. I was curious to know whether the characters she'd played were persistent, lingering in the mind long after the game was done, or whether it was more of an episodic shrugging on and off of character-as-costume, something more like the experience of a bit-part actor.

For Stark, larp is predominantly "a mode of personal discovery, a way of investigating my own psyche; the character I play is an internal manifestation of my own personality." This ties in with the literary outlook of her own academic background, perhaps; what Stark enjoys about larp is that hard-to-define "art experience," the kick of inner enlightenment she recalls first encountering while reading Woolf's *The Waves*: "it was like [Woolf] was explaining things about me to myself."

Not everyone plays this way, though. Boffer players tend toward a 'compartmentalised' approach to character, wherein the disconnect between the player's identity and the character's is more pronounced. In *Leaving Mundania*, Stark discusses a handful of larpers who deliberately step into personalities very different to their own when playing. For some, this is perhaps for the thrill of being able to commit illicit acts in a space where the consequences of those acts won't cause any real harm, much like a computerised war sim; still others seem to use their characters as a safe space in which to come to terms with traumatic experiences from their real lives, to walk in the shoes of others for a little while.

Given Stark's background, her metaphor – that boffer is to Nordic larp what genre fiction is to literature – makes a certain rough'n'ready sense. But the distinction is a little invidious: 'literature' is a moving target, after all, and there is a spectrum of literariness within almost every genre of any maturity.

Hence I'd modify Stark's terminology by swapping out 'genre' for 'pulp'; the latter, I feel, more fairly captures the exuberant disregard for high-art values and favouring of escapism and fun which characterise both boffer larp and popular / populist genre fiction, and makes of larp's various forms a contiguous spectrum rather than a binary split.

The highly influential larp *Mellan himmel och hav*, for instance, has all the hallmarks of science fiction's more literary aspirations –

unsurprising, given it drew on the works of Ursula K Le Guin, who is many things, but no writer of pulp. The commercially successful Stateside boffer campaign *Knight Realms*, by contrast, is pure pulp adventure: a cosplay theme park that convenes periodically to embody the generic Extruded Fantasy Product familiar from Terry Brooks's interminable Shannara franchise.

We can turn to literary criticism for a yet more useful analogy. E M Forster's *Aspects of the Novel* [12] was a core text of the modernist literary project, and while much of what it proclaimed as duty is now questioned as dogma, it contains some distinctions that remain useful. The one that applies here is the 'flat character' / 'rounded character' dichotomy: flat characters are predominantly defined by a single trait, which makes them "memorable, predictable and pure" [13], while round characters have a "want or need that makes them capable of change" [ibid, p. 96].

The flat character is a staple of the sitcom, the episodic serial: "[s]ince they are incapable of change, flat characters can go on and on and on, having an endless sequence of adventures." [ibid, p. 95] The round character is, at least in part, one of the concepts hiding behind the shibboleth of literature; their changes of nature as they progress through the story are what critics mean when they talk about 'character-driven' fiction.

Forster's dichotomy is often framed as a value judgement (round = literature = Nordic = good; flat = genre = boffer = bad), but that judgement inheres more within the critical canon than Forster's original formulation. If we think of flatness and roundness as different narrative strategies, the split becomes complementary instead of antagonistic: flat characters are ideal to escape into, avatars for enjoyable fictional journeys wherein the exterior is privileged and foregrounded; rounded characters, by contrast, focus the narrative on the interior, forcing the reader to engage with events at a more personal level, privileging philosophy and contemplation over escapism and fun.

Despite favouring the elitist aesthetic a literature over the rompy fun of pulp, I don't believe either is inherently better than the other; they are too different to bear the weight of that comparison, as are their larp equivalents.

This Is More Than A Game

It is tempting to view the wildly different natures of Stateside boffer larp – the rubber-swords-in-the-woods fantasy romps – and the Nordic art-house scene in terms of sociopolitics, not least because the majority of people I've spoken to on the topic have made the point before me, in some cases quite bluntly. Eleanor Saitta, a security consultant who's been a participant in the Nordic scene for some years, suggests that the demands of the Nordic school of gameplay – the willing surrender of an element of your consciousness to a collective experience, rather than simply playing a 'flat character' from off the peg – is "maybe a little too socialist in character for your average American."

Indeed, with its growing catalogue of worthy (if occasionally blunt-edged and sensational) experiments in experiential dystopia, the Nordic school of play looks to be, at a very abstract level, an explicitly political project that leans leftward, interested in reflecting reality with a view to interrogating the truth of the human condition, and perhaps to improving it with the knowledge brought back.

Boffer larp, at the other end of the spectrum, looks like pure escapism – about as political as dressing up with your neighborhood gang on Halloween. But Stark suggests I'm looking for boffer's politics in the wrong place: it's not in the game's content so much as its structure. In her paper "We Hold These Rules To Be Self-Evident: larp as metaphor for American identity" [14], she advances the theory that the original tabletopper RPGs (and the boffer fantasies that are their direct descendants) can be read as The American Dream in ludic form,

"an idealized vision of the archetypal immigrant's journey in which no one is left behind and everyone inexorably rises in stature. Boffer larp does more than reflect American values; national values structure the game."

Boffer larp's reliance on large casts playing in large outdoor spaces means that money matters start raising their heads early on, and there's an argument to be made that this – plus the legendary litigiousness of the United States – is inimical to the more arty or experimental forms of larp. Once your monthly game has become a business, there are bottom lines to meet... and regular customers to keep happy. A set-up like *Knight Realms* won't play a 'world-ender' plotline; why risk killing the golden goose if it's still laying?

Hence the episodic nature of such campaigns: each installment comes loaded with threat and jeopardy, but the game-world is 'rebooted' between episodes, returned to a stable state ahead of the next disruptive narrative. As with an series of cookie-cutter fantasy novels, there's always another volume, full of locations and characters you already know, and experiences for which you have some sort of precedent – not to mention the expectation of enjoyable escape from reality.

Boffer larp, then, like pulpy fantasy fiction, could be considered a project that neutralises the threat of Otherness by familiarising certain limited examples of Otherness within a fictional space whose intrinsic Otherness is sufficiently familiar. As an imaginative act, it demands a number of layers of separation between the player's true identity and their played character: you are playing not only someone who isn't you, but you're playing a someone who you could never be, among people you could never meet, in a world that is explicitly not the one in which your true identity resides.

The Nordic style, by comparison, delights in keeping the layers of separation as few and thin as is possible: characters that are a warping or expansion of the player's own personality, played in a world that (with varying degrees of abstraction or symbolic reduction) reflects the one within which it is nested.

Or, to put it another way: trad larp takes an individualist approach, wherein the players – equalised / normalised, at least in theory, by the complex rules and stats surrounding character generation and interaction – must make their own mark on a imaginary world that was designed specifically for them to make a mark upon. Nordic play, by comparison, is interested in character as changed and influenced by the game's narrative.

Inside / Outside

"The very first thing you need to do once you start playing this game is to choose your highest hope. If you have one, choose a better one. If you can't, don't play. In this game, you are supposed to create a new moral standard, and the choice is part of the gameplay. If you start with an old highest hope, how can you expect to have a new morality and new idea of what is good?" - Ari-Pekka Lappi [15]

The quote above is taken from an essay entitled "Playing 'Thus Spake Zarathustra'." Lappi's choice of the seminal philosophical text on walking away from mainstream morality is telling, set as it is amongst accounts of games which, to a greater or lesser degree of abstraction, attempt temporary walkings-away of exactly the type that Nietzsche was interested in. Consider Emma Wieslander's *Mellan himmel och hav*, which simultaneously critiques gender essentialism while immersing its players in feminist theory, making them experience a different spectrum of gender as something more than a *gedankenexperiment*, and *System Danmarc*, the cryptofascist urban dystopia; these are not outliers.

Other recent or in-progress games include *Kapo*, set in a prison run by its own inmates; *Dublin2*, another dystopia, based on EU immigration policy; *Valve*, a persistent campaign in the Helsinki region wherein shadowy conspirators literally kidnap other players, bundling them into vans pulled up on the hard shoulder. In 2011, a game called *Just a Little Lovin'*, exploring the impact of AIDS on the New York gay scene of the early Eighties, came in for a public drubbing in the Swedish newspaper *Expressen*, albeit a tame one by US or UK tabloid standards.

If the tragedy of AIDS is not shocking enough, then the does-what-it-says-on-the-tin-ness of *Gang Rape* is guaranteed to get both ends of the left-right spectrum in a panic. Part critique of rape culture, part experiment in ludic mechanics, its designer openly declares "don't play this game unless you're in a good place mentally, and really think you are up for it. *It is not meant to be fun to play.*" [16]

Society conditions us to view play of any sort as inherently childish, and Nordic larp challenges that assumption by literally, playing around with the biggest and most serious questions of all. There's something deeply – and, to some, disturbingly – postmodern about Nordic larp's more ambitious games. The entire scene, the philosophy, is saturated with the recognition of the subjectivity of experience and identity, but this is seen neither as boon or bane: it's just the default political assumption of its predominantly young demographic. Hence Nordic larp looks to me both leftist and utopian, but it's a young individualist sort of leftism, informed by Marx but not kneeling at his feet: a network-native take on identity fluidity which, perhaps, could only have emerged in small stable nation-states with a strong social security system.

Larp presents a toolkit for exploring that postmodern morality landscape, as well as tools for building bridges and dismantling the roadblocks encountered therein. The Norwegian larp organisation Fantasiforbundet has been working with the Peace & Freedom Youth Forum in Ramallah, Palestine, in the hope that they might not only bring a new form of imaginative play and entertainment to young Palestinians living under the shadow of conflict and oppression, but perhaps also to show how pretending to be someone else can bring an understanding of their experience and outlook which may have been lacking before. Perhaps this is what Holmas meant when he spoke of larp "changing the world"; I share his hope, if not yet his optimism.

Boffer larps, by comparison, seem to fail at modeling our more insidious social ills in a useful way. Of the long-running *Knight Realms*, which features the usual fantasyland panoply of humanoid sub-races, Stark reports that

> "[i]n-game racism also produces liberal-minded anxiety. Although racism is written into the game, the concept that all men, dwarfs and gypsies were created equal is hard to shed. [...] In other words, few players practise the racism dictated by the rules maybe because tolerance is so ingrained in players out-of-game, maybe because racist assumptions — even imaginary ones — create real-life discomfort." [17]

The phenomenon is intriguing, but I find myself wondering if Stark isn't wearing rose-tinted lenses here; couldn't the failure to 'play' the game's racism be rooted in the players' recognition of the mutual privilege they share outside the game? Does racism – remnant of our tribalist instincts that it is – perhaps feel wrong when directed at someone who you know, at some level, to actually be one of your own?

I make no solid claims, here, because I don't feel I can defend them using only secondary sources. But Stark's discussion of the more workaday sexual disparity in *Knight Realms* offers a supporting riff:

"... despite the game's strong female population, few women have achieved titled in-game power. In the course of the game's thirteen year history, there have only been a small handful of female knights – six out of about forty – and only two women have been appointed ladies of the land, out of about twenty-five appointed lords, though five women have married into noble titles in-game." [18]

There's little sign of liberal hand-wringing over that particular manifestation of privilege... if people are unwilling to play world-appropriate racism in *Knight Realms*, why isn't there a similar hesitation over world-appropriate sexism? After all, feudal states aren't exactly known for their enthusiastic enfranchisement of women, while our understanding of racism in similar settings is more limited.

Perhaps it's partly down to the American liberal psyche, which has internalised the existence and wrongness of racism, but which still struggles to see the ubiquitous influence of kyriarchy in the social fabric. Perhaps it's partly because, in the case of the gender disparity in *Knight Realms*, the physical trigger of the character's otherness – her femininity – is likely to be explicit in the physicality of the player. By contrast, you wouldn't get the same triggers for racist responses from the non-baseline-human characters in *Knight Realms* because, beneath the layer of make-believe, they still look just like One Of Your Lot.

Or perhaps these issues don't crop up in boffer larp because that's not what people play it for. In this, it lies close to its roots in American re-enactment groups. "The intent of re-enactment," explains a former Sergeant 1st Class of the US Army, who uses larp and re-enactment as 'safe zones' in which he can explore his post-PTSD outlook on the world, "is not to offend but to entertain, enlighten and educate." [19] Elsewhere, another re-enactor mentions his group's refusal to perform Nazi salutes or fly swastika banners, despite the otherwise obsessive attention to detail of the hobby. Some things, apparently, are just a step too far.

But perhaps not so for the Nordic school.

The Scene That Documents Itself

"When larping, we are given the chance to test out things we cannot or should not do outside of the safe frames of the game. If I had been in a situation similar to this in real life, I would have fought these feelings with my ethics, my intellect and my ideals. But because it was a game, I could let these emotions and impulses show me what kind of a person I hope never ever to become.

And that knowledge, and the process by which it was gained, was a hell of a high." [20]

Nordic larp is both a godsend and a curse to a writer; there's enough source material to drown in. The peripatetic Knutepunkt conference has been producing books that collect the best papers of the year into one place, and many of them are freely available as PDFs; in the last few years, videos of the paper presentations have been appearing on YouTube. There is, naturally, a wiki. There's enough primary material floating around to form at least a dozen doctoral theses, and that's before you even start looking at interdisciplinary intersections.

That said, you'll want to do a proper search of the literature before you begin. The academic influence on larp is clear to see in its nomenclature, in its intense self-theorisation; indeed, the scene is already producing its own larp-focused PhDs. True to its network-culture demographic, however, the openness and conviviality of the Knutepunkt circuit stand in stark contrast to the more staid conferences of the liberal arts, resembling science fiction fandom conventions – an important nursery for larp of all types – far more than literary symposia; open discussion and dialogue are not just important to the scene, but central to it. It's as if the community itself is a collective author, a gestalt entity – an interesting counterpoint for an artform where authorship is inherently unstable and slippery.

All this would be of some note even if larp were just another branch of the plastic or narrative arts as we already know them. What's fascinating about larp is its seeming potential: all art could be considered software which interacts with the localised cultural operating system running on the platform of our minds, but larp goes one step further, achieving its aesthetic affect by kludging, amending or outright rewriting that code – hacking it, in other words. If mainstream larps are the equivalent of the homebrew software BBSs of the Eighties, developing and sharing new games to play on their newly-accessible hardware, then perhaps the Nordic school are equivalent to the FOSS hacker hardliners, trying to see how completely they can *pwn* the machine. Pure diversion and escapism have been sidelined somewhat in favour of philosophical and ideological exploration. The language of theory is everywhere, including many scene-specific coinings and neologisms: 'narrative bleed' (not always as undesirable as it might sound, apparently); 'diegetic briefings'; 'fictional positioning'; 'formal transparency'. 'Metagaming'.

Nordic larp seems to be evaluated primarily in terms of its design (in which sheer scale or operational expense play roles minimised or inverted from those they play in the boffer mainstream), its theoretical daring or sociopolitical controversy, the level of affect induced in players, or a combination of all three. Fun is fine, of course, but out on the experimental edge it takes a back seat.

Like other artforms before it, larp has spawned its own little academy. Perhaps its techniques and rhetorics will spread, osmose into other disciplines, metastasise – become another conceptual toolkit through which we can observe, interrogate and manipulate the world, and ourselves-in-the-world.

Stockholm Syndrome

"The rules-light nature of Nordic games keeps the illusion of the game world intact." [21]

The growth years for tabletop RPGs saw more than a few morality scares based around the timeworn concerns of the baseline puritanical, and boffer larp stands ready as target for more of the same: the identification with and / or acting out of world-views that are false, deviant or outright Evil (where 'Evil', as always, refers to the morally untenable as defined by the moral majority). People imagining themselves to be something other than Americans – well, what more could you possibly want to be? There's something fundamentally unAmerican about wanting to be anything other than American, after all (indeed, it's the contradiction under the weight of which the constructed American identity is currently collapsing)... and anyway, pretending to be someone else is kid's stuff. Or maybe girlie-stuff. Certainly not man-stuff.

Stretch these imaginative exploits out all the way to Nordic levels of reconceptualising the self, though, and there's something even more terrifying – not just to the mind of Middle America, but to hierarchists everywhere. Viewed from atop the ivory tower of governance and control, larp techniques start looking a fair bit like indoctrination or brainwashing tools – tools whose use should be regulated, if not outright banned. (The authorities, of course, may continue using them to defend Our Freedoms; Big Brother knows best.)

These tools are, like all technologies, neither good nor bad – but nor are they neutral, per Kranzberg. Even though a chisel isn't a weapon, it can cause harm when used carelessly, and I find myself wondering what sorts of accidents we might see when arrivistes start rummaging around in the larp toolbox just for the lulz. After all, Stark and others tell tales of real-world relationships destroyed (and created) by the shockwaves from in-game events, and of sexual orientations reassessed in the wake of the more ambitiously sociopolitical games.

Stark suggests that "intense larp gameplay creates an altered state of consciousness" and as I read game-design papers from the Knutepunkt circuit I kept hearing echoes bouncing back from Timothy Leary's psychedelic theories of "set and setting". Implicit in both is the idea that not only is the mind plastic, but that experimenting with that plasticity is something akin to a duty, a possibility for personal development that shouldn't be passed up by those brave enough to take the plunge and step outside of themselves; a willing step toward becoming one's own post-Nietzschean ubermensch, if you like. So we might say that the Nordic larp scene is pioneering the development of a new toolkit for meddling with identity and empathy; a non-invasive intervention methodology based on consensual manipulation of environmental triggers and narrative framing.

Stark remains confident that the risk of psychological splashback is pretty low, thanks in part to the design of the Nordic games, with their pre-game workshops, safe-words and debriefings, but thanks also to human nature: "larp can't release something in you that isn't already there", she says, and mentions the Nordic scene's practice of selective ostracism, which is in part intended to keep risky or problematic players at arm's length from the hardcore stuff: people deemed 'unsuitable' are not encouraged to return, not embraced by the community.

My concerns linger, based on a rather bleak and cynical view of the sort of behaviours that, regrettably, are already there in most ordinary people, buried under layers of social protocol and the keeping-up-appearances of modern civilisation. I ask Stark what she thinks a disastrously failed larp might look like. "We already have a great example of that, actually," she replies. "Have you heard of the Stanford Prison Experiment?"

Everything is a game

"I'm not sure I felt this at the time, but in retrospect, I think my trip to Knudepunkt could be termed an elaborate larp built for one, a larp conducted in public without the knowledge of those around me, a pervasive game..." [22]

I'm left with the same feeling as Stark, without having yet so much as played a Nordic game or attended a conference: once you know what a larp can be, then everything starts to look like one.

Furthermore, there's a realisation that the psychological phenomena which larp explores and manipulates might just be the missing link between a whole bunch of artforms, technologies and philosophies. Perhaps it is the ubiquity of the toolset in use, namely the human imagination, that lends it this interstitial quality: conceived in reductionist terms, Nordic larp is simply imagination-as-play.

Where does experimental theatre end, and consensual indoctrination into a covert ideology begin? Can a temporary intentional community, in and of itself, be a form of performance art? Can a performance art piece become a political movement instead of just a statement? These questions pivot on the fluid dualities of fiction and reality, of reader and subject, which can be upended with a flick of the wrist or a twist of the frame; if we assume alter-modernism to have accepted and integrated (if not fully approved of) the ubiquitous ontological hollowness of the postmodern condition, then might Nordic larp be one of the first truly altermodernist forms, an experimental laboratory for the breeding of new metanarratives?

Maybe, maybe not. But Nordic larp's brisk defrocking of essentia-list identity politics, and its repeated demonstrations that convincing and compelling constructs of allegiance and collective identity can be assembled with surprisingly minimal effort, mark it out as a meta form. If a larp is a group of people playing certain roles in a certain imagined context toward some sort of goal, then larp itself – Nordic larp, the school, the movement – is a larp of larps, a metalarp; a game of games.

Larp has more obvious and more commercial cousins, of course. Alternate reality games use the same immersive world-overlaid-upon-world techniques, but the narrative is hierarchical, goal-orientated, and – ideally, at least for their creators – bounded by clear arcs of story which are defined before the game even begins; cosplay is busily turning dressing up and acting out as fictional characters into an acceptable (and in some cases praiseworthy) pastime for those over the age of eight; MMOs like World Of Warcraft have made the essence of the boffer larp experience less exhausting, weather-proof and post-geographical – play when you like, for as long as you like, with fellow players from anywhere in the world.

And then there's Second Life, the notoriously not-a-game synthetic world, which is the closest thing to Nordic larp online: Second Life gives you the space to build your imagined world, and the power to reimagine yourself as anyone or anything, but what you do with that potential is entirely up to you.

(It is perhaps telling that Second Life – wallowing deep in the "Trough Of Disillusionment" [23] now that the corporate Fortyniners have moved on – suffered terribly from would-be users not knowing what they were meant to do with it. If so, it may be equally telling that the communities that have survived and thrived there – the Wastelands, for instance, which is essentially an ongoing and pervasive post-apocalyptic larp community that meets exclusively in SL – are the ones that used the framework to build their own worlds, games and narratives within it.)

I've already compared genres – or rather the communities of discourse and canon-generation that take place within and around a generic label – to larp; genres are identities, after all, groupings of people as much as (if not more than) they are groupings of works or ideas. No contemporary discussion of identity and allegiance would be complete without a mention of Anonymous; as such, I'd offer that Anonymous is nigh indistinguishable from a persistent larp set in a territory that maps almost seamlessly to the world in which it is suspended. There's only one character you can play, and there's no GM to tell you how to play it. For Anonymoids, as for Second Lifers, code is law, as Lawrence Lessig put it: if it can be done, then you may do it. [24]

But the counterculture has no monopoly on larpish behaviour. I'd also contend that the nigh-viral *Six Sigma* [25] framework of manufacturing quality assurance took on very larp-like characteristics, especially as it trickled down – poorly understood and richly overhyped – to the very same small businesses that its progenitors were busily eviscerating in the mid- to late-Nineties.

Imagine a larp designed to explore perfection and efficiency in the workplace, being played earnestly by a handful of converts among a workforce of disinterested and disenfranchised NPCs who haven't had so much as a sip of the kool-aid... Well, perhaps I'm being unfair, here, but *Six Sigma* looked to me like an RPG for middle management long before I knew what Nordic larp even was.

Last but not least, larp bears more than a passing resemblance to a post-geographical evolution of Hakim Bey's Temporary Autonomous Zone: [26] polders and pockets scooped briefly out of consensus reality, wherein the normal rules of behaviour are suspended or rewritten. The European soundsystem-rave circuit of the 1990s, the Burning Man festival in the States, squats and communes and refusenik pseudocommunities like *Slab City* [27]:

they all play with(in) the world in a larpish way, which is to say they find a place in which to make of it a stage, sweep it clean of association, and improvise their roles upon it, unbound by any rules other than those agreed to among the players.

Herein, then, lies the terrible beauty of larp's promise: you can play whatever rules you like, whenever you like, wherever you like.

All you have to do is define them.

Game Theory

It turns out that the Nordic larp scene is more aware and engaged with its own intrinsic risks than I expected – not only the psychic-backlash potential of the immersion in otherness, but the subject matter too. Unsurprisingly, the Stanford Prison Experiment is a touchstone for both.

In his paper "The Golden Rule Of Larp" [28], Simo Järvelä declares the eponymous ethic to be "things *informed adults do consensually amongst themselves* are acceptable" (emphasis in original), and the Knutepunkt books, which function as a rough'n'tumble annual academic journal, burgeon with ethical navelgazing – some serious, some playful – alongside deconstructions and rakings-over of old games, successful or otherwise; the scene is always looking to improve, enhance, expand the boundaries of what larp can do. Taking care of the players – taking care of each other – is a big motivator, an elevated sense of communal responsibility and mutual support that, again, reminds me very strongly of the the raves and warehouse-party scene of the Nineties here in the UK: the shared acknowledgement of risk, the shared thrill of an adventure outside of mainstream reality, are powerful bonding agents.

To an onlooker, the "amongst themselves" bit is the most

interesting component of Järvelä's formulation, because within it can be found the seed of that ostracism, the very necessary outsiderdom of larp. Either a larp is played away from all other non-players or, as in the geographically or temporally larger 'persistent' games, among mundanes who are oblivious to the game's context. The scene is lucky in the former respect, as the Nordic countries retain their ancient 'right to roam' statutes, which frees up vast expanses of countryside for play without permission (and may well explain why all sorts of larp are so much more commonplace there by comparison to the States or the UK).

But when playing amongst non-players, the possibilities for problematic leakages between realities become clear. It's easy enough to restrict players from interacting with mundanes, but in a highly-charged and public scene – a chase through a shopping precinct, say, or a kidnapping – there's always the possibility of a bystander breaking through the fifth wall by accident, which could lead to all sorts of grief for all concerned. Järvelä candidly admits that this risk has yet to be fully quantified, let alone planned against – but his framing of the question (and its implicit plea for further discussion) is more like an earnest fanzine letter than a chin-stroking ethical polemic.

One suspects such developments will always be forced by events; in its newness, its enthusiastic experimentation and its occasionally narcissistic self-regard, Nordic larp looks destined to encounter any number of Rumsfeldian unknown unknowns. The only way to test the rules is to play the game.

This test-to-destruction approach, combined with Nordic larp's fascination with the deeper emotions, have led to the development of some fascinating game mechanics. Tabletop play still tends toward dicerolling, and there are a variety of approaches to boffer combat (including, in some cases, the requirement that an injured player method-act the effects of their imaginary injury as fully as possible); mainstream games less focussed on combat might use a combination of memorised statistics, cards drawn by chance or stone-paper-scissors hybrids to model interactions like an attempted theft or bluffing past a guard. But the Nordic scene adores abstraction, especially when modeling the affairs of the heart: Stark's account of playing *In Fair Verona*, for instance, a love-larp that required its players to interact via the medium of tango, is as strange as it is charming.

Emma Wieslander, author of the aforementioned *Mellan himmel och hav* and one of the scene's more prolific academics and theorists, is also the inventor of *Ars Amandi*, [29] a larp game mechanic or system for the safe simulation of love and sex which underpinned her groundbreaking game. *Ars Amandi* essentially maps the entire body onto a limited area thereof – arms, shoulders, sternum, upper back, neck below the ears – where touching is permitted. It sounds like an actor's workshop exercise (which is exactly where Wieslander got the idea from), but it's still powerful stuff, and *Ars Amandi*'s impact can be seen rippling through the last decade of Nordic larp, with articles and papers and workshops spreading the idea, challenging and refining and reapplying it.

The fame of *Mellan himmel och hav* is well-earned; not only does it still stand as a flagship experiment in political larp design and the deconstruction of gender, but it combined larp with other 'higher' arts – theatre, light art, music by contemporary composers. Most fascinating to me, however, is what happened after the game had finished.

The Way Out Is Through

"... none of these things seemed to have any meaning. Maybe these ideas I had about who I was weren't as important as I thought they were, and maybe I didn't need to be any of these things. But if so, how could I still be me? More than that, if these identities were something I could put on or take off at will, if all identity was fluid, how could anyone have an identity at all? [...] I was definitely in the middle of some sort of existential quandry." [30]

Mellan himmel och hav left lingering marks on its players, and on its creator. After the game ended, a number of players were unwilling to return to the social structures of consensus reality, with its institutionalised loneliness, its crude gender binaries, its doctrines of consumption for consumption's own sake.

So they didn't return – or rather, they only returned halfway, carrying over the communalism of the game into reality. A handful of them crammed themselves into an apartment meant for a single occupant; the need for personal space had been exposed as a myth, a narrative seemingly designed to drain money (and, by extension, time and passion) from the individual in thralls to it. Living together meant they needed less income, which meant everyone could work less – much less. This left time to spare for the true work: the exploration of a new mode of living.

"I guess that, in regards to the lifestyle, it was the other way around for me," Wieslander tells me by email.

"I have never felt comfortable with the heteronormative nuclear family, I guess; I find it a nuisance. Not only is the idea of autonomous individuals grouped together in too-small-to-be-functional groups scientifically unnatural to the human species, it also seems to me to be morally indefensible: it's a guilt-trap where most people are set up to automatically fail, but it also seems to be one of the cornerstones of gender-based discrimination.
So for me, making Mellan [...] was about taking that big 'what if?' and really trying it out. If gender roles are human constructs, we should be able to deconstruct and reconstruct at will – and as it turned out, we could! But as it's virtually impossible to deconstruct the gender binary without having a go at twosome partnering; that had to be part of the package, too.
It turned out to be a greater epiphany to many of the participants than they'd thought. I guess there wasn't a conscious decision on anyone's part to take the game out of the box so much as the experiment having a great impact on people, on both participants

and others.
A few months later there was another game set in the Swedish green-
wave seventies, playing a communal lifestyle with very much the
same set of players. I think it was a reaction to the alienation many of
the players felt in the 'normal' world, and a longing to go back to the
community that we constructed in order to establish the high level of
trust that was needed for the experiment to work."

It was a passing allusion to this very story that first piqued my interest in Nordic larp. What would it take, I wondered, what sort of depth of experience would you need to have in order to come back to reality and decide you were going to rewrite the role of your own life?

With hindsight, the connection is obvious, though it might not be so to someone who never rode the UK raves'n'festivals circuit of the Nineties. It's the Temporary Autonomous Zone effect, the euphoric sensation of having escaped without moving: having seceded, somehow, stepped sidewise out of a mainstream culture that marginalises or demonises you. I can recall any number of times when I was sat among a bug-eyed circle, with junkyard tablas tapping Morse over the top of industrial-strength techno just past the hedge or over the next hill, every breath held tight like a nervous dove at a peace rally as dawn starts to stain the edge of the sky, then loosed all at once in wordless triumph as the sun rises on a world that looks at once smaller and far bigger than it ever has before, and thinking it would be wonderful, wouldn't it, if we could live like this forever?

Wonderful might not be quite the word, of course – indeed, the outgoing Tory government of the time had set in motion the *fait accompli* annihilation of the travelling lifestyle, and was busy luring rave culture out of the black economy and into expensive (and, more importantly, legal) nightclubs. But it's worth remembering that *people still do this*: they drop out, they join cults or movements (or bands), they live in squats or on the road or in nameless permaculture ghost-villages far from civilisation.

And what else have they done, then, if not swapped the societal software suite with which they'd been inculcated for one they've modified to their preferences? That the new software is based on a historical social paradigm or an entirely imagined one is irrelevant; the hardware will run any software that's coded well enough to compile. Design yourself a different life: draw a door in the air, and step through.

Of course, you'll run into friction whenever your new set of rules puts you in conflict with others – especially those who aren't playing the game, and who may well view your game as dangerous, treacherous, blasphemous or insane. And so you modify and tweak and hack, adjust the game so it fits into the cracks where the rules of the non-players don't penetrate so thoroughly. You go interstitial.

And you realise, in the process, that the non-players aren't non-players at all.

They're just playing a different game.

Larp, the Universe and Everything

The response of John Major's Tories to the flourishing of rave culture was one of horror and disgust, akin to finding one's serene ornamental arboretum infested with tribes of manic squirrels toting boomboxes; much as a part of me would quite like to see secessionary sub-cultures gestated in larp and birthed into consensus reality, I suspect I've already seen the sort of reaction they will provoke from the players of the more popular game. (Nietzsche might have recognised it, too.)

But the world is fecund, full of interstices. Entropy sneaks into our software as well as our hardware, and the The Biggest Game is too big and complex for the gamesmasters to patch every bug right away. Gradual iteration would be the key, I guess: start with the small things, change slowly enough that the neighbours won't notice you any more than they notice the plane trees at the edge of the pavement adding sneaky inches of xylem and phloem. Think of it as an inversion of the boiled frog metaphor, where everyone else is the frog, warming up all unknowing on the outside of your jar... and before you know it, you've got the seed of something like the anarchic 'unlicensed sectors' of Delany's *Triton*. [31]

You'll have to be careful, of course, to boil the frog very slowly indeed, lest the licentiousness and liberty of your polder be accused of succouring our epochal bugbear, terrorism. Second Life suffered a similar fate during its time atop the Peak of Heightened Expectations, back in late 2007; its unregulated sprawl of freeform simulation space looked – to those who look for such things, and who tend to find them wherever they look [32] – like an infinite digital agar plate awaiting a sneeze of seditious sputum.

(The irony being, of course, that Second Life *was* a hotbed of terrorism, albeit a memetic and pop-cultural terrorism. Indeed, recalling the rampaging mobs of phallus-spawning faux-furry trickster avatars [33] controlled by 4Chan and the SomethingAwful goonswarms – a few unprotected fucks further down the family tree from Anonymous – you might even argue that Second Life really was a training ground for one of the most successful international terrorist (dis)organisations of recent history.)

The fear of the refusenik Other validates the notion of culture-as-larp: to conceive of the threat presented to mainstream cultural stability by the potential of people to reprogram themselves or each other, one must make the tacit admission that 'stable mainstream culture' is not a natural state – nor a stable, nor even a mainstream one – but is itself an ideological construct, a pervasive larp into which most people in a given region have been indoctrinated by default.

Where authority sees horror, I see some little hope, like Holmas: might larp let us literally play our way to more equitable social structures? It might, at the very least, let us test out adjustments to the one we've got.

"[Knutepunkt] evoked in me the yearning to return to that terrifying and fascinating place where there were no boundaries or rules, where there was no self, where identity itself seemed impossible. I felt as though I had peeked over the precipice of human existence, and in that one moment I was terrifyingly, truly alive." [34]

It occurred to me at a very late stage in the drafting of this essay that I've been blind to the most obvious comparison for the larp experience, namely the experience of being a child: the period in your life when starting an open-ended larplike game is as simple as saying to a friend "I'm Metatron, you're Starscream," and running away.

(The trigger for this particular epiphany was novelist Tim Pratt, whose tweets about his toddler son are a wonderful window into a mindstate I barely remember.)

So perhaps I've put the cart before the horse, here: Nordic larp isn't building a new toolkit for mindhacking so much as it is exploring an old forgotten mindstate we all once shared, rediscovering the completely immersive and freeform nature of play as experienced in childhood, and retooling it for an adult context. Childhood is when we assimilate the protocols of society; it's the pre-game workshop for the larp that is our lives.

So how about larp as a sort of software transhumanism? An ongoing project to transcend the limitations of the human, but not by hacking the body, nor even the brain, but the *mind*? Exploiting the recently-revealed plasticity of our thought patterns and social engrams; rooting and rebooting yourself into the imagination-theatre of childhood, then holding down F8 so you can fiddle around with the BIOS, install a different OS, tweak the power management settings...

It's a sweeping metaphor, I'll grant you, and only time will tell whether Nordic larp will make any measurable difference to

205

human civilisation as a whole, even as it makes a huge difference to the individual lives it touches. But I maintain that larp's implicit lesson is true: canonical consensus reality is, in effect, a roleplaying game that we're all playing, and so involved in that we've forgotten that the rules are all our own creation.

So: who do you want to be today?

First published on *Rhizome* in three parts between September and December 2012. Available online at http://rhizome.org/profiles/paulgrahamraven/.

PAUL GRAHAM RAVEN is a Research Assistant in Future Infrastructure, University of Sheffield (Pennine Water Group), as well as a science fiction writer and critic, rogue essayist-for-hire, ham-fisted post-rock guitar player and scruffy mountebank. He is Editor-in-Chief and Publisher of Futurismic - near-future science fiction webzine.

Notes

[1] Cf. Cory Doctorow, "Norway's new Minister of International Development is a D&D champ who thinks LARPs can change the worlds",in *Boing Boing*, March 27, 2012. Online at http://boingboing.net/2012/03/27/norways-new-minister-of-inte.html.

[2] The Institute for Collapsonomics (http://collapsonomics.org/) defines Collapsonomics "The study of economic and state systems at the edge of their normal social and economic function, including preventative measures to avoid destructive feedback loops and vicious cycles." Cf. also "Author! Paul Graham Raven meets the collapsonomics crowd", in Arc, 2012, online at http://arcfinity.tumblr.com/post/17709229968/author-paul-graham-raven-meets-the-collapsonomics.

[3] Lizzie Stark, *Leaving Mundania: Inside the Transformative World of Live Action Role-Playing Games*, Chicago Review Press 2012.

[4] Stark 2012: 56.

[5] Stark 2012: 234.

[6] "The annual Knutepunkt conference, first held in 1997, has been a vital institution in establishing a Nordic role-playing identity, and in establishing the concept of 'Nordic larp' as a unique approach." From *Wikipedia*, http://en.wikipedia.org/wiki/Knutepunkt.

[7] "Dzikie Pola (Wild Fields) is a Polish role-playing game, set in the historical setting of the 17th century Polish-Lithuanian Commonwealth. It had two editions: first in 1997 and second in 2005". From *Wikipedia*, http://en.wikipedia.org/wiki/Dzikie_Pola_(role-playing_game).

[8] Emma Wieslander, "Portraying Love and Trying New Genders", in *Nordic Larp Talks*, May 16, 2010, online at http://nordiclarptalks.org/post/604458190/portraying-love-and-trying-new-genders.

[9] Juhana Pettersson (ed.), *States of Play: Nordic Larp Around the World*, Pohjoismaisen roolipelaamisen seura 2012. Online at www.nordicrpg.fi/wp-content/uploads/2012/03/states_of_play_pdf_version.pdf.

[10] "*The Wheel of Time* is a series of epic fantasy novels written by American author James Oliver Rigney, Jr., under the pen name Robert Jordan. Originally planned as a six-book series, *The Wheel of Time* now spans fourteen volumes." From *Wikipedia*, http://en.wikipedia.org/wiki/The_Wheel_of_Time.

[11] Stark 2012: 214.

[12] *Aspects of the Novel* is a book compiled from a series of lectures delivered by E. M. Forster at Trinity College, Cambridge in 1927, in which he discussed the English language novel. Cf. E. M. Forster, *Aspects of the Novel*, Penguin Books 1980.

[13] Stephen Koch, *The Modern Library Writer's Workshop: A Guide to the Craft*

of Fiction, New York, Modern Library 2003.

[14] In Pettersson 2012: 171.

[15] Ari-Pekka Lappi, "Playing 'Thus Spake Zarathustra,'", in Pettersson 2012: 72.

[16] Emphasis mine. Cf. http://jeepen.org/games/gr/.

[17] Stark 2012: 132.

[18] Ibid.

[19] Stark 2012: 151. PTSD stands for Post-Traumatic Stress Disorder

[20] Elin Nilsen, "High on Hell", in Pettersson 2012: 11.

[21] Stark 2012: 240.

[22] Stark 2012: 234.

[23] The "Trough of Disillusionment" is the third phase of the hype cycle as theorized by Gartner, Inc.: the one in which technologies "fail to meet expectations and quickly become unfashionable." Cf. *Wikipedia*, http://en.wikipedia.org/wiki/Hype_cycle.

[24] Lawrence Lessig, "Code Is Law. On Liberty in Cyberspace", in *Harward Magazine*, January - February 2000, online at http://harvardmagazine.com/2000/01/code-is-law-html.

[25] "Six Sigma is a set of tools and strategies for process improvement originally developed by Motorola in 1986 [...] Six Sigma seeks to improve the quality of process outputs by identifying and removing the causes of defects (errors) and minimizing variability in manufacturing and business processes." Cf. *Wikipedia*, http://en.wikipedia.org/wiki/Six_Sigma.

[26] Hakim Bey, *T. A. Z. The Temporary Autonomous Zone, Ontological Anarchy, Poetic Terrorism*, Autonomedia, 1985, 1991. Online at http://hermetic.com/bey/taz_cont.html.

[27] Cf. Jason Motlagh, "Slab City, Here We Come: Living Life Off the Grid in California's Badlands", in *Time.com*, February 3, 2012, online at http://www.time.com/time/nation/article/0,8599,2105597,00.html.

[28] Simo Järvelä, "The Golden Rule Of Larp", in Pettersson 2012: 20.

[29] Cf. www.ars-amandi.nu.

[30] Stark 2012: 237.

[31] Samuel R. Delany, *Trouble on Triton: An Ambiguous Heterotopia*, Bantam Books 1976.

[32] Paul Raven, "The metaverse: bad for marketing, great for terrorism?", in *Futurismic*, August 1, 2007, online at http://futurismic.com/2007/08/01/the-metaverse-bad-for-marketing-great-for-terrorism/.

[33] Xeni Jardin, "Second Life griefers assault real estate millionaire Anshe Chung", in *Boing Boing*, December 21, 2006, online at http://boingboing.net/2006/12/21/second-life-griefers.html.

[34] Stark 2012: 241.

Honor Harger

Drone's Eye View: A Look at How Artists are Revealing the Killing Fields

209

James Bridle, *Drone Shadow 002*, Kemeraltı Caddesi, Istanbul, 09/10/2012. Made for "Adhocracy", part of the 1st Istanbul Design Biennial. Image courtesy the artist.

The unmanned aerial vehicle (UAV), or drone, has become one of the most potent weapons of contemporary warfare. Remotely controlled by operators thousands of miles away from the theatre of war, drones carry out aerial attacks which leave hundreds of people dead. The increasing amount of 'collateral damage' from US drone strikes on the Pakistan-Afghanistan border, recently lead prominent politician, Imran Khan, to lead a high-profile protest against their use. [1]

Artists have been actively documenting the impact of the use of drones in warfare for some years now. Trevor Paglen's *Drone Vision* (2012), recently on show at Lighthouse in Brighton, provides us with a chilling "drones-eye-view" of a landscape, enabling us to see what drone-operators see.

The utterly compelling and disturbing film installation, *Five Thousand Feet is the Best* (2011) by Israeli artist Omer Fast, tells the story of a former Predator drone operator, recalling his experience of using drones to fire at civilians and militia in Afghanistan and Pakistan. At one stage of the film, he describes the use of what marines refer to as "the light of god", the laser targeting marker, which is used to direct hellfire missiles to their intended target. [3]

"We call it in, and we're given all the clearances that are necessary, all the approvals and everything else, and then we do something called the Light of God – the Marines like to call it the Light of God. It's a laser targeting marker. We just send out a beam of laser and when the troops put on their night vision goggles they'll just see this light that looks like it's coming from heaven. Right on the spot, coming out of nowhere, from the sky. It's quite beautiful." [4]

Writer, publisher, web developer and artist, James Bridle responded to this by creating his own work, *The Light of God* (2012).

Sharing Paglen and Fast's concern with the use of drones in warfare, Bridle has crated a series of projects which attempt to reveal their presence in the landscape. His *Drone Shadow* (2012) interventions are one-to-one representations of the MQ-1 Predator Unmanned Aerial Vehicle (UAV) drawn to scale within urban landscapes. The first was drawn in London this February (in collaboration with Einar Sneve Martinussen), and the second in Turkey this October as part of the Istanbul Design Biennial.

Like Paglen and Fast, Bridle's work stems from a deep concern with increasingly invisible and seamless military technologies that are creating the context for "secret, unaccountable, endless wars".

Bridle writes:

"the drone also, for me, stands in part for the network itself: an invisible, inherently connected technology allowing sight and action at a distance. Us and the digital, acting together, a medium and an exchange. But the non-human components of the network are not moral actors, and the same technology that permits civilian technological wonder, the wide-eyed futurism of the New Aesthetic and the unevenly-distributed joy of living now, also produces obscurantist "security" culture, ubiquitous surveillance, and robotic killing machines. [...] We all live under the shadow of the drone, although most of us are lucky enough not to live under its direct fire. But the attitude they represent – of technology used for obscuration and violence; of the obfuscation of morality and culpability; of the illusion of omniscience and omnipotence; of the lesser value of other peoples lives; of, frankly, endless war – should concern us all." [5]

His latest work, released last week, is *Dronestagram* (2012). Bridle has been collecting images of the locations of drone strikes, and sharing these photographs on the photo-sharing site Instagram. His intention is to make these locations more visible, bringing them closer to us, and in the process perhaps making the reality of the daily occurrence of deadly drone strikes more tangible. [6]

He utilises public records from the Bureau of Investigative Journalism [7] which document strikes as they happen in Pakistan, Yemen or Somalia. After confirming the location of a strikes, he then uses Google Maps to create a satellite image of the targeted location. The image, accompanied by a description of the site, and the death-toll, if known, is uploaded to Instagram.

The images of deserted, barren landscapes and abandoned buildings have a sobering potency juxtaposed with with the banal pictures of pets and parties that populate Instagram. But it is what we don't see that gives these images such an emotional power: the mortality. Bridle writes:

"drones are just the latest in a long line of military technologies augmenting the process of death-dealing, but they are among the most efficient, the most distancing, the most invisible. These qualities allow them to do what they do unseen [...]. Whether you think these killings are immoral or not, most of them are by any international standard illegal." [8]

The work of artists such as Trevor Paglen, Omer Fast, and James Bridle exists within a long tradition of artists bearing witness to events that our governments and military would prefer we didn't see. But Bridle's work is also part of an ongoing collective effort from both artists and engineers to reveal the technological infrastructures that enable events like drone-strikes to occur.

As technology becomes more ubiquitous, and our relationship with our devices becomes ever more seamless, our technical infrastructure is becoming ever more invisible. When our environment becomes opaque or invisible, it becomes difficult to interpret it, and act within it. As artist and critical engineer, Julian Oliver recently noted, "our inability to describe and understand technological infrastructure reduces our critical reach, leaving us both disempowered and, quite often, vulnerable." [9]

Or as Bridle puts it, "those who cannot perceive the network cannot act effectively within it, and are powerless. The job, then, is to make such things visible." [10]

This post originally appeared on Honor Harger's website *Particle Decelerator.* Published on *Rhizome* on November 13, 2012. Available online at http://rhizome.org/editorial/2012/nov/13/drones-eye-view-revealing-killing-fields/.

HONOR HARGER is a curator from New Zealand who has a particular interest in science and technology. She is currently Artistic Director of Lighthouse (www.lighthouse.org.uk), a digital culture agency in Brighton, UK. Prior to working at Lighthouse, Honor was guest curator of the transmediale festival in Berlin, and from 2004-2008, was director of the AV Festival in the North East of England, the UK's largest biennial of digital art, film and music. From 2000-2003 she was the first curator of webcasting for Tate, where she also curated events and concerts at Tate Modern. Her artistic practice is produced under the name r a d i o q u a l i a together with collaborator, Adam Hyde. Honor is slightly obsessed by science. She writes the blog, *Particle Decelerator* (http://decelerator.blogspot.com), which collects together news from the worlds of science, art and technology, placing a special emphasis on the collision between the quantum and the cosmological.

Notes

[1] Cf. Glenn Greenwald, "US detention of Imran Khan part of trend to harass anti-drone advocates", in *The Guardian*, October 28, 2012, online at http://www.guardian.co.uk/commentisfree/2012/oct/28/detention-imran-khan-drones.
[2] The video is available online at http://vimeo.com/47723379.
[3] The video is available online at http://vimeo.com/34050994.
[4] Quoted from *Five Thousand Feet is the Best*, 2011.
[5] James Bridle, "Under the Shadow of the Drone", in *Booktwo.org,* October 11, 2012, online at http://booktwo.org/notebook/drone-shadows/.
[6] Cf. http://dronestagram.tumblr.com/.
[7] Cf. www.thebureauinvestigates.com.
[8] James Bridle, "Dronestagram: The Drone's-Eye View," in *Booktwo.org,* November 8, 2012, online at http://booktwo.org/notebook/dronestagram-drones-eye-view/.
[9] In Jason Huff, "Artist Profile: Julian Oliver", in Rhizome, September 5, 2012, online at http://rhizome.org/editorial/2012/sep/5/artist-profile-julian-oliver/.
[10] James Bridle, "Under the Shadow of the Drone", in *Booktwo.org,* October 11, 2012, online at http://booktwo.org/notebook/drone-shadows/.

Jordan Crandall

Drone Desire

Image courtesy the author

Nestled amid the sagebrush along the California side of the U.S./Mexico border is a small DIY drone airfield. Makeshift and unkempt, devoid of pavement and infrastructure, it is unremarkable in the absence of the gathered assemblies of amateur pilots, planes, and spectators for which it is intended. One might well overlook it, yet perhaps in some way it serves as a model of sorts, a harbinger of airports to come: a preview of what drone airfields might look like, writ large, in their absence of traditional control platforms and optical infrastructures. Much like this one, the unmanned airport would contain no centralized control tower presiding over the runway and no lighting tracks reflecting its contours. There is no need for a commanding view from above. The distributed and windowless drone, devoid of any interior, requires no human sightline for its flight. In an operational sense, its trajectory is not visual. Geometries of looking, whether from a cockpit or a control tower, have been replaced by networks of sensing. Interior / exterior relations, at least in any conventional, spatially-continuous sense, diminish in their structuring relevance.

The demand for unmanned vehicles is not limited to state agencies. Civilians, too, want their drones. Weather researchers want to send them into storms to gather data. Energy companies crave their use for geological surveying and pipeline monitoring. Security companies want to send them up for traffic monitoring. Farmers, for crop dusting. Ranchers, for livestock tracking. Commercial upstarts yearn to service them and train their operators.

Perhaps the most visible drone desire is that of the everyday consumer. Homegrown drones sprout up everywhere, their production and operation facilitated by an expanding network of hobbyist groups and blogger communities. Ignited by their prominent roles in sci-fi literature, television, and film, drones populate social and cultural imaginaries. They appeal to generations of gamers, who relate to the control interfaces through which they are operated and the first-person-shooter style images that are streamed from them, often accessed on the very same computer screens upon which these games are played.

Drone display flourishes out of backyards, streets, abandoned lots, and open fields, and in the consequent posting of video and photographic documentation on social networking sites. There is an erotic dimension to the sharing, acquisition of expertise, and demonstration of prowess that these sites enable. One might build drones because, as one suburban teenage DIY blogger boasts, they are a "chick magnet."

Drones are curious, kick-ass, and cute. They embody a potent combination of menace and allure. The wavering light of mystery, the harsh precision-target glare; the flickering transmission and the transcendent stare. As there are entire websites devoted to the drone's fetishization as an object, there is a growing body of interest in its destruction and disappearance: drone crash lore.

The erotic fascination comes from both the effective drone striking and the failed one being struck. The pilot and the hacker. The friend and enemy. Exultant drones that gleam against a clear blue sky jostle with downed ones, however real or virtual, that explode in sprays of parts.

Stories are woven around downed drones and their sites however accurate they might be or outrageously fabricated they might seem, and enfolded into all manner of drone sightings, stagings, and speculations. Captured drones are decked out in nationalistic finery, commanded to act in the service of ideals, helping to bolster public support and consolidate allegiance. As drones are outgrowths of the histories of UFOs and robotics, as they have been integrally tied to warfare, war technology, and anxieties of invasion, however real or fictional, at least since the mid-twentieth century, the inevitable corporate and national spin that is woven around the accident and its aftermath is often, as with mid-century UFO crashes, seen as a coverup or conspiracy. Drones are reported to belong to secret military programs in the testing stages. They hover in the sky and then just vanish, like quivering projections of our unease. They embody fears of our human limits, and desires of our transcendence. Some believe that advanced stealth drones have been developed by reverse-engineering the flying saucer that crashed near Roswell. (It's a small step from the unmanned system to the out-of-body experience: the domestic abduction to the alien one.)

False specters – lawless, renegade? Genuine news items or outright charades? Stories propagate with little or no verification, especially as they activate the imaginary, affirm ideological orientation, and offer easy munitions in wars of attention. They amplify or diminish in scale and intensity as they become harnessed to personal anxieties, beliefs, and desires, aligned with group imaginaries and ethical codes, and enabled by communications platforms. They might create new conflicts or fuel existing ones, produce new images and dreams, rearrange or reinforce existing routines.

Drones slamming into Sunni political headquarters in Mosul, Iraq. Nose-diving into the Wales airport runway. Striking power lines and cutting off power in Alberta Canada. Vanishing into Pakistan's tribal region in North Waziristan. Plummeting into uninhabited terrain near Ghanzi, Afghanistan and the Indian / Pakistani border. Collapsing into the Gaza Strip. Plunging into the Mojave Desert. Disappearing into Turkey's desolate Mardin province. Cannonballing into the coast of Spain. Ditching into the Iraqi countryside. Rolling with scrub brush across the rough desert terrain near Indian Springs, Nevada. The Italian Air Force has discovered one of its downed drones floating along the surface of the Adriatic Sea, its body glistening in the sunlight like the bleached skin of a whale.

If a demo reel of Oscar-worthy drone crash moments were assembled – perhaps in order to pitch the drone for a starring role in the ubiquitous action-adventure movie – it would be composed of clips like these. In true commercial fashion, it would seek to harness the drone's potent combination of desire and threat. Like any good object of desire, it would give us what we want and what we fear. As a conduit of identification and affect, it would allow us to extend ourselves, in all our sensory acuity, into a landscape devoid of everyday political rationales and ethical or moral judgments: to plunge headlong into the melee.

The resulting drone crash action-adventure documentary would be geared for the everyday viewer primed for the economies of disaster, of pleasurable violence transmitted on private screens – sites where drone games are played and drone missions consumed. Its trailer might go something like this. Ground control operators have suddenly lost control of an armed Reaper flying a combat mission over Afghanistan. A manned U.S. Air Force fighter is dispatched to shoot down the renegade drone before it flies beyond the edge of Afghan airspace. (In the world of robotic warfare, human pilots are apparently still good for something: shooting down wayward drones.) The tension builds: disciplined man against chaotic unmanned.

The fighter plane arrives too late. The renunciant Reaper, speeding headlong into its own future, crashes into the side of a mountain. Abstracted in a shower of engine oil, smoke, lost data, and crushed composites, its dissipating fuselage drops. Amplified in a rush of sensation and adrenaline, its absorbing body elevates.

Perhaps the doomed drone performs a more vital function than the exultant one. It destabilizes the coherency of the vehicle and embroils it in a politics that was heretofore invisible or diminished. At the onset of the crash, the drone and its component material and discursive actors, occasioned by the reverberations of the event, are catapulted into a more public space, rendered newly exposed and available for affiliation. A twisted geometry of spilt forms and unmasked roles, of networks sought and broken, the drone now offers itself to connection, continuity, and salvage. The agential components of event and drone become newly active in their negotiations. The catastrophe reveals an agential dispersal: the network of the negotiation.

Yet at the same time, revealing the elements with which actors and events affiliate in order to maintain their centrality and force, the catastrophe orchestrates a consolidation. It stabilizes relatively coherent or consistent forms that embody or heighten the specifics of the crash site, the actor, the part, rendering it singular, bounded, and unique. The drone crash, both materially and discursively, is an event that both disrupts and congeals the dynamic. It provides an exception, but also an amplification. It dislodges conventional associations, allowing hidden infrastructures to be revealed and new ontological frameworks to take shape. All kinds of novel players enter the scene. The drone cannot be reassembled in quite the same way.

Published on *Rhizome* on February 20, 2012. Available online at
http://rhizome.org/editorial/2012/feb/20/drone-desire/

JORDAN CRANDALL (http://jordancrandall.com) is a media artist, theorist, and performer. He is Professor in the Visual Arts Department at University of California, San Diego. He is the 2011 winner of the Vilém Flusser Theory Award for outstanding theory and research-based digital arts practice, given by the Transmediale in Berlin in collaboration with the Vilém Flusser Archive of the University of Arts, Berlin. His current project, *UNMANNED*, is a blend of performance art, political theater, philosophical speculation, and intimate reverie. It explores new ontologies of distributed systems, and the status of the human in a militarized landscape increasingly dependent on automated technology. The work was developed in a residency at Eyebeam center for art and technology in New York City and most recently performed in 2012 at V2_ Institute in Rotterdam.

222

Giampaolo Bianconi

Robopix

Two screenshots from Timo Arnall, *Robot Readable World*, 2012. Video, 05:09. Online at http://vimeo.com/36239715.

In 1971, Michael Snow spent five days atop a lonely mountain in North Quebec. He was making a film, or supervising a film that

224

was being made by his robotic companion, depending on how you think about it. The film that robot made is called *La Région Centrale*: over the course of three hours, the machine runs through all its programmed motions, capturing every possible view of the barren mountain. Certainly, at least some of the images would have been overlooked by a human filmmaker.

Despite its lack of human warmth, Snow's film retains a mystical slant: the film is somehow purer for being supposedly unpolluted by the artist's direct physical control over the camera, and the machine bears witness to a primal landscape with nearly cosmic objectivity. The saintliness of *La Région Centrale* was possible not only because it played off of the machine's lack of learned perception (the machine couldn't find beauty in a landscape or respectably frame a shot), but also because the machine couldn't process the landscape as information.

Timo Arnall's short film *Robot Readable World* (2012) investigates the exact opposite: how robot-eyes gather information from the cityscapes, mediascapes, and people. [1] On display in the video are the brightly colored squares, rectangles, circles, and lines that recognize cars, faces, doors and everything else that robots see. In our contemporary security-obsessed climate, robots and computer vision are tasked with growing responsibilities to survey urban and rural environments. Instead of following Matt Jones' suggestion that "instead of designing computers and robots that relate to what we can see, we meet them half-way – covering our environment with markers, codes and RFIDs, making a robot-readable world," [2] these machines read a world without man-made markers permitting robo-legibility.

As Antje Ehmann describes in her notes to Harun Farocki's similar video *Eye / Machine II* (2002), "The traditional man-machine distinction becomes reduced to 'eye / machine,' where cameras are implanted into the machines as eyes." [3] Now that machines can see, what do they see and what do they make of it?

Farocki's video uses footage from the Gulf War, when the covenant between visual technology and the military was finally sealed, to test the answers of these questions. From Ehmann:

"It has been said that what was brought into play in the Gulf War was not new weaponry but rather a new policy on images. In this way the basis for electronic warfare was created. Today, kilo tonnage and penetration are less important than the so-called C3I cycle which has come to encircle our world. C3I refers to Command, Control, Communications and Intelligence – and means global and tactical early warning systems, area surveillance through seismic, acoustic and radar sensors, radio direction-sounding, monitoring opponents' communications as well as the use of jamming to suppress all these techniques."

Unlike the cliché of *Terminator* vision, in which images are translated into text for the benefit of a human audience, these computers with robot eyes have no need for a human alphabet. When the images involve text, they're there for human benefit, allowing us to interface with the machine and make sure the robot is seeing things correctly. The machines themselves don't need text: they rely on algorithmic data to understand the world they see. Whereas Snow looked to his mechanical filmmaker for almost godlike neutrality, Farocki and Arnall use their videos to begin understanding the agenda behind seeing machines. Whereas Farocki highlights the affects of robotic vision on warfare, Arnall concentrates on surveillance. Both show how, less than 50 years after *La Région Centrale*, the concept of a movie made by a robot has gained far more sinister implications.

Unlike *La Région Centrale*, what's fascinating about *Robot Readable World* is watching robots collect data. Consumer technologies that use extensive algorithms to predict what humans want, something like Netflix or auto-tune, already have built in data to modulate its response. Kevin Slavin [4] offers a good overview of algorithms and the role they play in society. In these contexts, algorithms are designed to create and maintain norms:

they produce a monoculture where everything becomes smooth and agreeable. Watching robots gather data from cities and streets, building an archive to be understood and maintained algorithmically, some of the questions that comes to mind are: what monoculture will this data produce, and how will it be enforced? What normative behavior is being coded, and what steps will algorithms take when faced with deviant behavior?

First published on *Rhizome* on June 21, 2012. Available online at http://rhizome.org/editorial/2012/jun/21/robopix/.

GIAMPAOLO BIANCONI is a regular contributor to *Rhizome*. His writing has also appeared in *Idiom*, *The Brooklyn Rail*, and *Modern Matter*. He lives in Brooklyn.

Notes

[1] The video can be viewed online at http://vimeo.com/36239715.
[2] Matt Jones, "The Robot-Readable World", in *Berg*, August 3, 2011. Online at http://berglondon.com/blog/2011/08/03/the-robot-readable-world/.
[3] Available online at www.farocki-film.de/augm2eg.htm.
[4] Kevin Slavin, "Those algorithms that govern our lives", Lift Conference, Geneva, February 4, 2011. Video documentation online at http://videos.liftconference.com/video/1177435/kevin-slavin-those-algorithms.

228

Adam Rothstein

On the Natural History of Surveillance

HE'S AFRAID OF SPIDERS.
HE'S AFRAID OF HORROR MOVIES.
HE'S NOT AFRAID TO SPEAK UP.

If you see a suspicious package, or notice odd behavior, don't be afraid to speak up. It will keep us all safe. Call (617) 222-1212 Text your tips to 873873.

If you see something, say something.

Massachusetts Bay Transportation Authority   massDOT

Upon hearing the phrase, we may not know exactly what a "cephalic sniffer" is, nor whether it is a real piece of technology. However, as to what such a nefarious device might be able to do, we could surely begin to imagine from the name alone. And as for whether it is technological reality (it is not, being invented by Philip K. Dick in his story *Clans of the Alphane Moon*), [1] from its "sci-fi" sounding alliteration we might guess correctly that it is purely fantasy.

At least it was fantasy when PKD invented it in 1964. Today, advances in biometric identification mean that while a device that can search out an individual by his or her brainwaves is not yet on the market (at least publicly), searching out a person by face or speech pattern is decidedly real. Furthermore, brain-computer interface devices (BCI) have been commercially available since at least 1999. [2] So how far are we from the technological reality of a biometric tracking system hacking BCIs and tracking individuals? If we change the name to "brainwave keylogger", [3] it suddenly is less fantastic, and frighteningly plausible.

Submitted for your consideration: an entire list of surveillance concepts, proposed by science-fiction stories. [4] Note the technologically real items: Augmented Reality, ubiquitous surveillance, drones, eavesdropping rays, and tracking systems. These are all things that we might call "cutting edge tech", but indeed, certainly real tech. Surprise, shock, uncanniness, paranoia – yes, it is repeated enough to be cliché – the future is here.

Aerostat Monitor - a small flying platform	Neal Stephenson (1995)
Agfom Potent-Shot - picture the future	Philip K. Dick (1964)
Alibi Archive - personal recording	Robert J. Sawyer (2003)
Anti-Spying Device	Isaac Asimov (1951)
Auto-Scan	Roger Zelazny (1966)
Bee Cam	Karen Traviss (2004)
Cephalic Sniffer	Philip K. Dick (1964)
Conductive Film - spray on wire	Jack Vance (1979)
Control Helmet	Edmond Hamilton (1938)
Copseye - a surveillance drone	Larry Niven (1972)
Crimestop - no dangerous thoughts	George Orwell (1948)
Deadman's Device	Patricia Jo Clayton (1990)
Deep-Radar	Larry Niven (1980)
Dog Suit - costumes for aliens that work	Roger Zelazny (1976)
Dornier - VTOL surveillance drone	William Gibson (1988)
Eavesdropper - check if it's safe	James Blish (1957)
Eavesdropping Ray - hears through walls	Ray Cummings (1930)
Electronic Locator	A.E. van Vogt (1945)
Electronic Spy	Clifford Simak (1952)
Eyes - semi-autonomous surveillance drones	Roger Zelazny (1966)
Floater Camera - fly and spy	Michael Crichton (1985)

Flying Eye - I see you	Harry Harrison (1959)
Genoprinter	John Varley (1977)
Great Ear	Philip K. Dick (1970)
Holo (License) - 3D driver's license	Alexander Besher (1994)
Housefly Monitor - flies with sensors	Philip K. Dick (1964)
Ident Darts -track your brain	Philip K. Dick (1969)
Ident-Key	Philip K. Dick (1964)
Invisible Watchmen	Edmond Hamilton (1938)
Lifelog - life record	Charles Stross (2007)
Little Bird - surveillance drone (UAV)	Greg Bear (2003)
Low-scale Detectors	Ray Cummings (1930)
Magnetic Eyes	John Jacob Astor IV (1894)
Monitored In-Home Security Camera	Jerry Pournelle (w/L. Niven) (1981)
Panic Alarm	Philip K. Dick (1968)
Photonomous - stay anon on Flickr	Cory Doctorow (2008)
Probe Screen Hood - block the penetration of the mind	Philip K. Dick (1955)
Profile Sniffers - sifting the web	Bruce Sterling (1998)
Psychoprobe - head examined	Arthur K. Barnes (1938)
Public Eye	Robert Heinlein (1982)
Public Iris Scanner - Mr. Anderton	Steven Spielberg (2002)
Radiant - just like RFID	Jack Vance (1954)
Radiant Shield	Jack Vance (1954)
Raytron Apparatus - aerial surveillance	Ray Cummings (1928)
Receptor Tape - very thin microphone	Jack Vance (1979)
Recording Eye - interplanetary surveillance	Robert Silverberg (1969)
Robot Snake Spy	Greg Bear (2009)
Robot Tracking Device - preferred surveillance tool of AIs	Philip K. Dick (1960)
Robotic Trash Can - watch it	Harry Harrison (1959)
Scarab Robot Flying Insect - tiny robotic insect	Raymond Z. Gallun (1936)
Senso-Cells - read the quirks	J.G. Ballard (1962)
Shere - beat the brain scan	Frank Herbert (1984)

SIN (Single Identification Number) - national ID	William Gibson (1988)
Skull Bug - implanted RFID monitor	Alfred Bester (1974)
Skyball	David Gerrold (1985)
Sky-Eye	Neal Stephenson (1995)
Solar-Powered UAV	Roger Zelazny (1980)
Sonomagnetic Fabric - listen with your shirt	David Brin (1990)
Spy Beam	Isaac Asimov (1951)
Spy Ray Goggles - see through walls	E.E. 'Doc' Smith (1934)
Static Field	Isaac Asimov (1951)
Stick-Tight	Jack Vance (1964)
Subphoton Search Ray - see through walls	Nat Schachner (1937)
Tattletale - predicts the ankle monitor	Philip K. Dick (1963)
Telescreen - Big Brother is watching	George Orwell (1948)
Tracer-Bird - the birdie watches you	Roger Zelazny (1980)
Tracing Glasses - find criminals now	Gosho Aoyama (1994)
Tracking Bracelet - a high security device	Patricia Jo Clayton (1990)
Traffic Control Camera - automatic identification	Robert Heinlein (1941)
True-Vu Lenses (Goggles) - sneak a peek	David Brin (1990)
Undercover Detective Robot - who am I?	Harry Harrison (1956)
Vibration Screen - keep spy beams out!	Nat Schachner (1937)
Video Unit - big bro	William Gibson (1996)
Voice-Changing Bowtie - hey, it's me	Gosho Aoyama (1994)
Webeye - Logitech endpoint	Larry Niven (1996)
Wristband Viewer	Roger Zelazny (1980)
Zed-Ray	Ray Cummings (1936)

But what is truly uncanny about our present "not-so-distant future", is that we continue to refer to it as the future. There is no need to speculate. We have a fully evolved culture of surveillance technology in the United States. Here is another list: this time of non-fictional surveillance concepts. They range from the slightly-troubling to the fully-horrifying, but they all are now employed by the government of the United States for the purposes of so-called "National Security":

Palantir, No-Fly List, Full Body Scanners, "If you see something, say something", Border Searches are Exempt from the 4th Amendment, Stop and Frisk, NYPD spying on Muslims, TSA harassment of children, the elderly, DHS spying on activists, That DHS exists, FBI terrorism entrapment, Domestic Drone Surveillance, Private Prisons, Over 1% of US Citizens in Jail, National Security Letters, FISC Courts, Immigration Policy, Abu-Ghraib Prison Abuse, Guantanamo Prison Camp, Extraordinary Rendition, Torture, Codifying Indefinite Detention, FBI seeking backdoors in electronic communications, ICE raids on websites, Iris scans of civil disobedience protesters, Warrantless Wiretaps, Recorded Future, The Domestic Communications Assistance Center [5]

Nevertheless, the primary means by which we engage with surveillance culture outside of the news media is still speculative art and fiction. Speculation allows us, as both creators and readers, to play design-fiction with reality. It is rapid prototyping in emerging psychological patterns. But these thought experiments do not exist in a vacuum.

Francis Ford Coppola – in the DVD commentary to *The Conversation*, his 1974 film about audio surveillance technology and the crimes to which it leads – expressed surprise that viewers interpreted his film as being about Watergate, an episode revealed in the same year:

"Not only was the script for The Conversation *completed in the mid-1960s (before the Nixon Administration came to power) but the spying equipment used in the film was discovered through research and the use of technical advisers and not, as many believed, by revelatory newspaper stories about the Watergate break-in. Coppola also noted that filming of* The Conversation *had been completed several months before the most revelatory Watergate stories broke in the press."*

Even in 1974, a film that attempted to realistically speculate about surveillance technology was surpassed by reality itself. The film becomes about Watergate, by nature of Watergate's reality.

That speculative art and fiction would be presaged by the reality it attempts to engage is not unexpected. The prescient author of speculative fiction, exploring near-future outcomes of technology with politically-expedient accuracy, is truly a public intellectual. Speculative work is hardly reducible to mere dystopic condemnation or fanatical futurism; it often forecasts and explores detailed and nuanced scenarios that would not be investigated as thoroughly without this speculation, nor with such a wide consumption among the public.

But there, lies the real question: why is it that speculative art and fiction – still relatively a niche production – is the only means of confronting and thinking about surveillance culture? It is not surprising that speculative art and fiction are currently best equipped to deal with reality. What is surprising is that the rest of art and fiction has not yet begun dealing with our systemic technological persecution.

This is "post-9/11" surveillance culture. Therefore, our growing surveillance state is not merely tied up with speculations on technology, but also with a neurotic response to a national trauma. Such a heavily-invested event within the cultural narrative of national history is a difficult thing to approach, regardless of one's political reaction to the event itself.

The heavy cultural wreckage to be assessed is visible, ringing the craters of nodes like the "Post-9/11 Novel". As a literary response to said event, this is a prefigured piece of art that had already been defined in the cultural narrative before it existed. Said Zadie Smith about the novel *Netherland*: the work itself is a cultural event in which a "literary form in long-term crisis" meets "a community in recent crisis." In other words, this post-9/11 book was, by its themes, already searching for the fantasy of the meditative "Post-9/11 Novel" like a bandaid for a scraped knee:

The stage is set, then, for a "meditation" on identities both personal and national, immigrant relations, terror, anxiety, the attack of futility on the human consciousness and the defense against same: meaning. In other words, it's the post–September 11 novel we hoped for. (Were there calls, in 1915, for the Lusitania novel? In 1985, was the Bhopal novel keenly anticipated?) It's as if, by an act of collective prayer, we have willed it into existence.

This sort of meditative novel's attempted subject is not speculation, nor the reality of surveillance, but an attempt to image reality via symbolism. Anxiety, suspicion, doubt, terror – all of these emotions are evoked in depth, piled up like so many *New York Times* cover pages saved for posterity. The problem with novels of this sort is the images become icons as they are cataloged and archived. As if in our recitation of these images, their symbolic power would allow us to heal. Writes Smith, "There was the chance to let the towers be what they were: towers. But they were covered in literary language when they fell, and they continue to be..." Rather than work through our psychological wreckage as human beings, we pile on the symbols, burying the site of our loss with symbolically overdetermined Freedom-Tower-style neurosis novels.

Meanwhile, more cameras are installed, more drones take to the air, more people-who-are-not-us are harassed at the border and on the streets, and our crime rate drops through the new everlasting-recession as we repress and oppress our cultural fears behind prison walls. We hide surveillance from our eyes, repressing it because this imaging technology is not under our control. The shadows grow behind our backs, in our recurrent speculative nightmares.

W.G. Sebald, in the introduction his book *On the Natural History of Destruction*, led his explanation of German literature's inability to deal with the aerial bombardment of the country during World War Two in this way:

"[...] when we turn to take a retrospective view, particularly of the years 1930 to 1950, we are always looking and and looking away at the same time. As a result, the works produced by German authors after the war are often marked by a half-consciousness or false consciousness designed to consolidate the extremely precarious position of those writers in a society that was morally almost entirely discredited. To the overwhelming majority of the writers who stayed on in Germany under the Third Reich, the redefinition of their idea of themselves after 1945 was a more urgent business than depiction of the real conditions surrounding them." [7]

It would be hard to argue that American authors and artists, post-9/11, are "almost entirely discredited morally", even if they ought to be. The cone of the blind spot is not turned into the past, like it was for post-war Germans. Instead, it is turned forward to the future. American culture leverages its future history on the empty symbolism of the event, closing its eyes in empty meditation, failing to perceive the undergrowth of surveillance culture upon the cultural agar plate. 9/11 trauma may not be the unilateral seed of surveillance culture, but it is the rich substrate upon which this growth has become endemic.

Because we can only speculate about it, we have trouble understanding surveillance culture as a massive, technological thought-holocaust that is interpolating our lives everyday, showing no sign of ceasing, and offering few ways of combatting it. We understand it only as an "act", that is sometimes done by some to others; always by good people to bad, or by bad people to good.

The actors are superheroes and villains, with an extrasensory grip upon these technologies, their deployment, and component ethical systems. They can "see the matrix", and bend and break its rules. Even speculative art and fiction – along with treatments in other genres like horror, spy fiction, and murder mysteries – treat surveillance as an act in the hand of a limited number of special actors. Surveillance is a conspiracy, a crime, a limited new technology, a merely-potential dystopia, a thing that, Jason Bourne willing and SCOTUS don't rise, would never happen to you and me at our suburban shopping outlet. But indeed, Target Stores is targeting you. [8] *This is not an isolated event or outlier, a conspiracy or a potentiality*: this is normal.

It may seem historically insensitive to compare surveillance culture to the aerial bombing of Germany, or any other act of widespread destruction. After all, we're not even talking about terrorist attacks or drone strikes themselves, but the juridico-discursive present in which the technological regime that treats human beings as data to be purged become accepted as commonplace. While the deaths are seemingly minimal, this is a long-tail horror. There is no Berlin in which all of this will eventually end, at which point we can make hypothetical arguments whether certain technologies were worth it, quantified in lives saved or surrenders negotiated. There is no bunker into which all Muslims, Sikhs, People of Color, immigrants of all ethnicities, and activists can go to shoot themselves and end this via a climactic Downfall Event – after which the United States government will have "won", and we can enter a post-war bliss. There is no Hiroshima to document by destruction, to photograph with a nuclear flash – after which we can open the internment camp doors, and eventually erect a monument to what was deeply regretted. There is only more surveillance, forever. There is only long and bureaucratic slow-genocide, a spreading morass differentiated only by another set of prison walls built around the last.

Sebald suggests that the only way for literature to deal with history is to treat those events as objective facts. In resorting to symbolism or other literary devices, literature becomes obsessed with its own symbolic value, rather than the preservation of history.

The ideal of truth inherent in its entirely unpretentious objectivity, at least over long passages, proves itself the only legitimate reason for continuing to produce literature in the face of total destruction.

Conversely, the construction of aesthetic or pseudo-aesthetic effects from the ruins of an annihilated world is a process depriving literature of its right to exist.

Truth, objectivity, and legitimacy are dead letters in an age of ubiquitous surveillance. Authenticity has, through irony and atemporality, become no more than a sigil of itself, another hollow tower built on the reality of wreckage. But there is still fact. We can create a terrain of facts on which to base our actions in the world, rather than only playing with interpretive metaphor, or the architectural models of speculative.

Fact is what we take as acknowledged, by integrating it to our worldview. For instance, if a character in a narrative gets on a bus, we expect the character to pay a fare. We do not take the bus fare as a pivotal moment in the narrative. There is no need to speculate on whether or not there will be a fare, or how much it will be.

Speculation is good, because it allows us to step outside of our assumptions about the world, and consider things differently. But once patterns of action have been accepted as facts, our speculation can tackle other issues. In this example, we might ask where the bus is going.

We have yet to fully acknowledge surveillance culture as fact. We are still wondering "what if we have a full blown technological surveillance culture?" The culture we have allowed to be built is towering above us, but the majority of art and fiction have yet to agree that it is even there. We speculate about it, and generate some interesting scenarios, that occasionally, become built into facts. But this is a slow way of dealing with reality.

And naturally, this means that the methods of revolt via the facts have yet to be determined. Because speculation, while boundlessly creative, is no revolt. And if our art and fiction have trouble visualizing a way to revolt, then what chance do our politics have?

239

First published on *Rhizome* on June 6, 2012. Available online at
http://rhizome.org/editorial/2012/jun/6/natural-history-surveillance/.

ADAM ROTHSTEIN is an insurgent archivist and writes about politics, media, and
technology wherever he can get a signal.

Notes

[1] Philip K. Dick, *Clans of the Alphane Moon*, Ace Books 1964
[2] Cf. *Wikipedia*, http://en.wikipedia.org/wiki/Brain-computer_interface.
[3] "Keystroke logging (more often called keylogging or "keyloggers") is the
action of tracking (or logging) the keys struck on a keyboard, typically in a
covert manner so that the person using the keyboard is unaware that their
actions are being monitored. It also has very legitimate uses in studies of
human-computer interaction. There are numerous keylogging methods,
ranging from hardware and software-based approaches to acoustic analysis."
From *Wikipedia*, http://en.wikipedia.org/wiki/Keylogger.
[4] The following list is taken from the website
http://www.technovelgy.com/ct/Science_List_Detail.asp?BT=Surveillance.
[5] In the online article, for each of these words the author provided a link to
an online resource. Cf. http://rhizome.org/editorial/2012/jun/6/natural-history-surveillance/.
[6] Zadie Smith, "Two Paths for the Novel", in *The New York Review of Books*,
November 20, 2008, online at
www.nybooks.com/articles/archives/2008/nov/20/two-paths-for-the-novel/.
The book discussed is Joseph O'Neill, *Netherland*, Pantheon 2008.
[7] W. G. Sebald, *Luftkrieg und Literatur*, 1999. Eng. trans. *On the Natural History of Destruction*, Notting Hill Editions, London 2003.
[8] Cf. Kashmir Hill, "How Target Figured Out A Teen Girl Was Pregnant Before
Her Father Did", in *Forbes*, February 16, 2012, online at
www.forbes.com/sites/kashmirhill/2012/02/16/how-target-figured-out-a-teen-girl-was-pregnant-before-her-father-did/.

Giampaolo Bianconi

Package Yourself

241

Ed Fornieles, *Characterdate.com*, 2011. Screenshot

At a time when so many Americans are disgusted with the personhood of corporations, it's surprising that more persons don't move to secure their expanded rights. Dan Graham notes,

> *"Jasper Johns was the first American artist to fully understand that the newly subjectivized advertising icon and the gestures of Abstract Expressionist painting – which struggled against the cultural domination of this new form – were virtually identical." [1]*

The place of the (white male) individual and his potential for transcendence had already merged with corporate strategy. Warhol began operations at his Factory in 1962, and by 1966 Foucault proclaimed that man "would be erased, like a face drawn in sand at the edge of the sea." [2] In 1978, the band Devo told *The SoHo Weekly News* that they'd decided to "mimic those who get the greatest rewards out of the business and become a corporation."

According to Bernadette Corporation, [3]

"Mock incorporation is quick and easy… no registration fees, simply choose a name (i.e. Booty Corporation, Bourgeois Corporation, Buns Corporation) and spend a lot of time together. Ideas will come later."

Bernadette Corporation was founded in 1994 as "the perfect alibi for not having to fix an identity." [4] Similarly, the Bruce High Quality Foundation employs a post-individual aesthetic while using the language of a endowed institution as opposed to a corporation. Yet the post-individual kernel is clearer in the Foundation's mission, which presents itself as the arbiter of the estate and legacy of "the late social sculptor" Bruce High Quality. The Foundation is founded on the negation of an already fictional identity. The Icelandic Love Corporation, based in Reykjavik, adopts the title of a corporation without jettisoning their identities.

Corporate art practice challenges stale narratives of contemporary art, which resuscitate themes and tropes of 20th century conceptualism. By claiming the featureless corporation as the active artmaker, BC and other similar façades maneuver around cliché and retreat from the individual artist-archetype: a character to be media-narrativized into a pop-psychological explanation of their noble craftsmanship or pathology of resistance.

Corporations, much like contemporary art, have a unique relationship with the iterable. In an essay discussing the irony of the corporate sponsors of the San Diego Zoo, critic and writer Chris Kraus explains, [5]

"Like contemporary art, corporate linguistics seeks to eliminate the dreary mechanics of cause and effect. Shit happens. People demand."

Corporate language rests on clichés that are instantly understood. Phil Spector reportedly wondered, "Is it dumb enough?" while listening to "Da Doo Ron Ron." The question that defined popular music has as much bearing on contemporary art: unencumbered by the boring (Kraus' "dreary mechanics"), only that which is instantly understood remains. That which is dumb enough.

The artist Ed Fornieles, whose work includes the trend-forecasting agency *Recreational Data* [6] and the management training company *Coaxiom*, indicated to me that part of what he likes about working with corporate aesthetics is the power of boring corporate cliché both in language and imagery. "Corporations have their own logic," Fornieles told me. "It doesn't always have to be about me." In a sense, engaging with corporate style makes transparent a generic corporate aesthetic – visible in promotional materials, architecture, offices, commercials – which is both recognizable and unfixed. What's appealing about something so blandly real is its ability to blend into the fabric of reality without the risk of a unique stake or identity.

In their 1996 video *The B.C. Corporate Story*, Bernadette Corporation uses of the structure and style of internal corporate mission videos while spouts generic corporate lingo about hard work, analysis, and markets over images of fashion photography before ultimately showcasing catwalks from BC produced fashion shows. "Makin' clothes, man... there's quite a lot to it," says the narrator in a Southern business monotone. BC's emphasis on fashion, corporate identity-forming art, emphases the double-bind selfhood as predetermined individual preference. BC member Antek Walczak remarked to Chris Kraus,

"What are people's problems with fashion? There's a blind spot – people think fashion is uniquely superficial, as if everything else is not." [7]

The video ends with the opening scene from *Blade Runner*. The invocation of *Blade Runner*, which depicts a world in which the Tyrell Corporation manufactures robots virtually indistinguishable from humans (known as replicants), takes the place of a traditional video-ending corporate mission statement. The tension of *Blade Runner* comes from Harrison Ford's own inability to know whether or not he is a replicant. The difference is imperceptible, what's important is that the Tyrell Corporation is a company that can create individuals, which is less a science-fiction speculation than a capitalist reality. Like Ford chasing the replicants, the battle-line between superficiality and authenticity has become variable to a degree that makes it negligible. Instead of fighting for semantics, it's preferable to become the Tyrell Corp. If having an identity is merely an excuse to be absorbed by consumer culture, the only sensible way to escape that assimilation is to align yourself with the corporate agencies of capital.

Bernadette Corporation's 2003 video *Get Rid of Yourself* is an anti-documentary featuring footage of the 2001 G-8 riots in Genoa. On their website, Bernadette Corporation describes the video as "an encounter with emerging, non-instituted or identity-less forms of protest that refuse the representational politics of the official Left." BC's goal here is to utilize the representational form of video without closing, halting, and commodifying the event as "something recognizable."

If corporations have potential in an aesthetic context, can art have a totally corporate form? In her essay "Indelible Video," [8] Chris Kraus compares the strategies of American Apparel to the strategies of contemporary art:

"The company's merchandising aesthetic includes the display of amateur-produced art that reprises – like much MFA art – reprises various landmarks in conceptual art of the past decades [...] Recruiting talented young women as both content-advisors and sex partners, [Dov] Charney creates a paradigm for how life can be lived a different way."

Kraus goes on,

"It could be argued that entrepreneurial ventures like American Apparel fill the void left by avant-garde process-art projects of the last century, which are no longer practical for artists who must maintain their careers [...] American Apparel resonates against the economic and psychogeographic state of the culture like a gigantic work of conceptual art."

What makes this argument so compelling is that a corporation's status as a for-profit enterprise does nothing to exclude it from the realm of high art.

As the Bruce High Quality Foundation mentions on its website, "Only Joseph Beuys and Andy Warhol compared in their conflation of art with the systems of modern media." Yet both of those artists couldn't escape the grasp of identity: endlessly psychologized, their strategies for dismissal of the self created an even greater aura of personhood around the place where the person should have been destroyed. Warhol tried to get rid of himself using the model of a Hollywood studio. Auteurism injected that model with individuality and personality. He should have looked to IBM.

First published on *Rhizome* on July 25, 2012. Available online at http://rhizome.org/editorial/2012/jul/25/package-yourself/.

GIAMPAOLO BIANCONI is a regular contributor to *Rhizome*. His writing has also appeared in *Idiom*, *The Brooklyn Rail*, and *Modern Matter*. He lives in Brooklyn.

Notes

[1] Dan Graham, "The End of Liberalism", in *Rock/Music Writings*, New York: Primary Information, 2012, 50-60. 55.

[2] Cf. "Foucault Funk: the Michel Foucault Postmodern Blues", 1997, online at www.theprofessors.net/foucault.html.

[3] Bennett Simpson, "Techniques of Today - Bennett Simpson on Bernadette Corporation", in *Artforum*, September 2004. Online at www.bernadettecorporation.com/introduction.htm.

[4] Quoted in Chris Kraus, "The Complete Poem/Bernadette Corporation", in *Where Art Belongs*, Los Angeles: Semiotext(e), 2011. 44-56.

[5] Chris Kraus, "Panda Porn", in *Video Green*, Los Angeles: Semiotext(e), 2004, 159-164. 163.

[6] Cf. www.recreationaldata.com.

[7] Quoted in Kraus 2011: 44-56.

[8] Chris Kraus, "Indelible Video", in *Where Art Belongs*, Los Angeles: Semiotext(e), 2011. 119-139.

Maura Lucking

The
Ephemerality
of IRL:
An Interview
with
Rob Walker

Omni Consumer Products, Fight Club Soap.
www.omniconsumerproductscorporation.com

"Tell me about yourself, and you might mention where you're from, the music you prefer, perhaps a favorite writer or filmmaker or artist, possibly even the sports teams you root for. But I doubt you'll mention brands or products. That would seem shallow, right? There's just something illegitimate about openly admitting that brands and products can function as cultural material, relevant to identity and expression. It's as if we would prefer this weren't true..." [1]

Journalist and author Rob Walker has a long history of projects that look at the intersection of designed objects and consumer behavior. Formerly of the Times Magazine "Consumed" column and currently found at Design Observer, Walker coined the term "murketing" in his 2008 book, Buying In: The Secret Dialogue Between What We Buy and Who We Are, [2] to describe the blurred strategy between marketing and entertainment used to sell products without the associations of an overt branding campaign. Walker's current project swings to the other side of the spectrum, examining brands so compelling they don't need physical manifestations: he has curated "As Real As It Gets" at New York's Apexart about imaginary brands and fictional products. [3] I talked to Walker over email about some of the questions the exhibition raises about our complicated relationship with things.

ML. The show, in many ways, seems like a continuation or a synthesis of your own speculative design projects with your different tumbleblogs. The majority of your own practice exists exclusively in the virtual sphere, for example your recent *Significant Objects* [4] project with Joshua Glenn, where thrift store detritus was listed on eBay along with fictive narratives of their history in order to demonstrate the subjectivity of value (and collected as a book earlier this year). In "As Real As It Gets" you bring these supposedly imagined objects into an actual space. What attracted you to this more traditional form of curating, and how do you see it as distinct from projects that live exclusively online or in publication?

RW. The honest answer to the specific question of what attracted me to the physical-space scenario for this project is that Apexart offered to let me organize a show! So the process sort of worked in the opposite direction: What could I do with this space? I had this longstanding interest in imaginary brands and fictional products and various art and design work that touched on those notions, and that seemed like it would be a particularly good thing to deal with in this way.

But to get at what I think you're really asking about, I suppose it's a matter of figuring out what works best for a given project. *Significant Objects* is an interesting example. Back when that was just a vague and unnamed notion, I actually imagined it as a gallery thing – you'd see the objects, the stories would be printed out and displayed, and there would be a live auction. But outside of being a visitor, the art / gallery world is a total mystery to me. So I didn't do anything about it until I hooked up with Joshua Glenn. By then it seemed obvious the way to do it was online. Not to be a big cliche about this, but the tools are there and available to all and easy to use: Wordpress to publish the stories, eBay to serve as the sales mechanism. We didn't have to ask anybody to let us do it, we could just do it. So there's that.

On the other hand, as that project took off, it did have physical-world offshoots – an event at Litquake in San Francisco, and more recently a book version collecting 100 stories from the project. But the book in particular was a different beast. It's tricky, because I've definitely had the experience of "you've seen this digital picture online, now here it is in a gallery, or a book," and it's actually disappointing. So everyone involved made an effort to avoid that. The book was published by Fantagraphics and designed by Jacob Covey, who did an amazing job of making this into something beautiful and lasting, something that needed to be a physical object. [5]

So things can sort of overlap or go back and forth. Even my stuff on Tumblr really varies by project. *Unconsumption*, [6] a group Tumblr I co-founded, is put together like a publication, with an audience very much in mind. I also have a thing called *Google Image Search Results* [7] that's basically an offshoot of a piece I wrote for *Design Observer*. That could evolve into something else, maybe. But the point is that online / offline also overlaps with subjects I'm dealing with as a writer vs. these other creative projects, whatever you want to call them. Most of my personal

Tumblrs are more like notebooks; I'm not thinking about the audience at all, I'm just collecting stuff I find interesting and sometimes patterns emerge from that, leading to something else – an article, a project. *The Hypothetical Development Organization* [8] can be traced back to something I wrote on my old blog, just saying "It would be cool if someone did X" (and then Ellen Susan and G.K. Darby said "yeah, us, let's do it!")

For this show, when I got that call from Apexart, I personally just thought it would be really cool to see all this work brought together in physical space, even though I'd seen images of a lot of it online. Of course we also added some more work through commissions, but even if we hadn't, to me it was definitely worth it not only to see these objects and images in person, but to see them together. Plus, we could add sound – the audio work inspired by *The Ladies' Paradise* that Marc Weidenbaum's Disquiet Junto musicians created. So it's really an experience to be in that space. I hope!

Anyway it was a great experience to do something in this kind of setting and I'd love to do it again, but until the next opportunity comes along, I can bide my time on the Web.

ML. It is easy to see the humor in the show – both as sardonic commentary and uncanny or unheimlich physical manifestations of products from fictional worlds (Staple Design's iteration of H.G. Wells' Tono-Bungay is kind of like a high art Duff Beer can). However, it seems like an over-simplification to just read these objects as satire. Do you see this collected body of work as a heightened version of our present consumer culture brought to its most extreme (but logical!) conclusion? Or is there some room for serious advocacy and futurism in the work as well?

RW. I think the uncanny point is the most important one to me. Interestingly one of the artists in the show, Shawn Wolfe, there's a book of his work called *Uncanny*. But the Tono-Bungay piece is a good one to focus on because Staple Design and I talked about this explicitly: We didn't want the result to read as satire or parody, we wanted it to look plausible, like the kind of thing a branding firm might really do for a real-world client. Only in the case the client is fictional, and in fact Tono-Bungay was invented by H.G. Wells as a kind of stand-in for untrustworthy products. So you have to really look closely to sort out what's going on.

So you mention Duff Beer, we have some stuff from The Simpsons in the show, and that stuff does read as parody – on the Krusty-O's box, there are worms in the cereal. So it's not plausible; at a glance, it's obviously satirical. The reason it's in the show is that when the Simpsons movie came out, they produced actual boxes of the stuff, put it in actual 7-11s, and people actually bought it. So it wasn't just a satire of consumer culture, it was an example of consumer culture. So that seemed like an interesting thing to include in the show.

In a way I think the show is less about consumer culture than it's about doing interesting things with the language and grammar of consumer culture, recognizing how powerful some of those tropes are and how we take them for granted and thus fail to take them seriously. So there's a lot in the show that looks familiar at first glance, but the more you look at it the more you realize something else is going on – and that this isn't familiar at all, it's very strange. Or uncanny.

ML. There is a fair amount of zombie media-looking stuff included – products designed to intentionally appear technologically outdated and, thus, looking like they have no place in functionally providing any service other than highlighting the failed utopianism of their design and, essentially, standing alone as branded commodities. What do these outdated and low-tech pieces say about the message of the show (whose exhibition design is itself an anachronistic sort of 1960s elementary school general store chic, itself a product placement for Blu Dot)?

RW. I think the answer here might vary depending on the piece. But maybe to follow up on the point above, I would say there's a lot in the show that's using design language and branding language to express ideas about people, human nature, faith in progress, and so on. And maybe doing so in a way that's more or less the opposite of how, for instance, retail environments work. The point of retail is really to make you stop thinking. And obviously something like Ryan Watkins-Hughes' *Shopdropping* cans, which he would insert into retail environments, that's there to interrupt that mindless process and jolt you into seeing: What is this? Someone could say that the intent there is to speak about consumerism, but I think it speaks about human behavior.

I'm not sure what to say about your description of the exhibition design! I can only say my goal there was that, particularly for some of the more product-y pieces, I wanted to avoid having everything on a traditional Art Gallery Pedestal; I was hoping to make the space feel both more accessible and maybe more chaotic and disconcerting. I had some contacts at Blu Dot and ran this idea by them – I thought it would be funny, just one more weird twist, to reach out to an actual company to loan us a few pieces for the display. I was actually really pleased with the stuff they suggested. And they had a sense of humor about the whole thing – I mean, the line "product placement courtesy of Blu Dot" is something I thought would be an interesting bit for the viewer to consider, but I wasn't sure they'd go for it, and they totally got it. Anyway, I think the final look was different without being gimmicky. (I didn't want to make the space look like a bodega or a boutique, I've seen that done and that's great, but I wanted the context to be something that wasn't particularly recognizable.)

Having said all that, to go back to your first question, this was something that was incredibly stressful for me – figuring out how to arrange the objects and images. The Apexart folks were really helpful, but it was just something I'd never thought about before in any serious way, and it was quite a challenge. It's a lot harder than picking a cool theme on Tumblr.

ML. Something is a little unsetting about the appearance of a 3D printer concurrent with all these branding and product design campaigns without a concrete physical form. While several of the campaigns cite professional, empirical evidence for their direction (more than one, interestingly, cite the writing of behavioral economist Dan Ariely) while the production system, the 3D Makerbot Replicator, a compact little desktop model made for casual "at home printing" is attempting to democratize a process that formerly required a high level of skill. What does this inversion of professionalization say about the current state of design?

RW. So when I had the first meeting with the Apexart crew, somehow the subject of 3D printing came up randomly. It was something they were interested in and I knew a fair amount about MakerBot because of an article I'd written. Then when I was putting together my wish list of stuff to pursue for the show, and I was thinking about Shawn Wolfe's work, I remembered at that one point he'd created this plastic "toy" version of his *Remover-Installer™*, the non-product non-sold by his imaginary not-brand BeatKit™. I looked up a picture of it to refresh my memory and it just looked like something that could be printed on a MakerBot machine. And, yes, that bringing that into the show could introduce another dimension to the whole idea. For one thing, we're producing a non-product, on site.

But also, if this whole show is about the intersection of imagination / fiction and brands / products, doesn't the rise of 3D printing actually have to be addressed somehow? Part of what the MakerBot people talk about is that, you know, you can use this thing to dream up your products and print them at home, instead of going to a big box store. There are various ways to respond to that notion, of course. But to push a little further in that direction: One of the events connected to the exhibition is a pair of MakerBot workshop sessions (one for kids, one all-ages) led by Liz Arum, who's in charge of their education outreach. This sort of opens up the whole concept of the show in a participatory way – you (or your kids) can come dream up your own fictional object and get it printed in the gallery.

ML. I appreciated your stab at an "exhibition trailer." Actually, I'd love to see those for more shows... But that leads to the question: do you have a brand strategy for the exhibition? If you did, what would it be?

RW. We intend to target key influencers across critical demographics who can leverage their social networks to maximize – Just kidding. The trailer, [9] as you've deduced, is not something that I particularly planned. I didn't know what I was doing, both in the sense that I have no training in making videos, and was just using whatever the editing software is on a MacBook Pro, and also in the sense that I put it together and then asked: Well, what is this? It's certainly not a document of the show, and it's not really an ad. It seemed like a Kickstarter video that wasn't asking for money. And then I decided it was like a "book trailer," but for an art show. And yes, having reached that conclusion, I agree, I think others should do that for art shows, particularly people who actually know how to make videos. I think it could be an interesting and useful category.

To the branding question: We did at one point talk about maybe making locally run ads for the show, but that never went anywhere. The only branding tactic I can point to is the giveaway objects, which was one of my favorite things about this entire process. Apart from postcards and a brochure for the show, there are a number of things people can just take from the gallery: Ladies' Paradise balloons, Veladone-RX pens, FutureWorld business cards, and Tono-Bungay stickers. All promotional objects for things that don't exist. And each conceived in a way that I hope it has some kind of life of its own after the show is over.

Which reminds me of one last point about the physical-space vs. online-space issue, actually. When I got to New York the day of the opening (I live in Savannah) and saw everything in real life, in that room, I was really blown away – it was just so much cooler in person than I'd imagined. (And I had high hopes.) But the next thing I realized was: Oh, wow, so five weeks from now, this will be gone! Which is totally different from a Web site. The *Significant Objects* site will be in place for as long as Josh and I care to keep it up, but "As Real As It Gets" will end on December 22. Downside of doing something IRL, I guess: It's more ephemeral.

First published on *Rhizome* on December 10, 2012. Available online at
http://rhizome.org/editorial/2012/dec/10/rob-walker/

MAURA LUCKING is a historian and writer on art, architecture and object culture based in Los Angeles.

Notes

[1] Rob Walker, "As Real As It Gets", Exhibition Essay, 2012.
[2] Rob Walker, *Buying In: The Secret Dialogue Between What We Buy and Who We Are*, Random House 2008.
[3] "As Real As It Gets", Apexart, New York, November 16 - December 22, 2012. More information and documentation of the exhibition is available here: www.apexart.org/exhibitions/walker.php.
[4] Online at http://significantobjects.com/.
[5] AAVV, *Significant Objects*, Fantagraphics 2012. With contributions by William Gibson, Sheila Heti, Jonathan Lethem, Tom McCarthy, Lydia Millet, Bruce Sterling, Scarlett Thomas, and others.
[6] Online at http://unconsumption.tumblr.com/.
[7] Online at http://pergoogle.tumblr.com/.
[8] Online at http://hypotheticaldevelopment.com/.
[9] Online at http://vimeo.com/54198170.

Cole Stryker

"Go to bed, Tao Lin."

Tao Lin's Eeeee Eee Eeee:
an example of good writing that doesn't need comparison

Steve lived in Orlando, Florida. His mom, Jan, was always at her sister's place—or wherever—playing Texas Hold 'Em, a kind of poker. She was going to Las Vegas soon, with her sister. Steve was twenty-four. He did not have a job. But he pretty much was raising Ellen and his other two sisters, who were seven and five or something. It was summer now so none of them had school except Ellen, who for some reason was taking summer classes—probably to try and make friends, Steve thought, which made him feel empathy. Most nights Steve and the people he went to high school with played video games or drank beer while playing poker; the same things they'd been doing for about seven years, and the future—or, rather, the past of some future's future, Steve thought suddenly—was just another thing that wanted to get away from everything else and finally be completed, which is to say that Steve himself had no future. The future was only itself, and it didn't care; it was somewhere else and it was already done, like bread in an oven. Steve felt very calm. He moved icons around on his computer for almost ten minutes, drew five whales with Microsoft Paint, closed the file without saving, went in the bathroom, washed his hands, smiled exaggeratedly at his own face for fifteen seconds and then watched a movie he'd already seen, ate something without paying attention to what it was, went to sleep, woke in the morning, made eggs for the kids—six in one skillet; he would email Andrew, he thought: "I cooked twelve eggs in one skillet and it looked like a cake"—played video games at a friend's house, came home, made dinner for the kids, watched TV, went in the bathroom, saw Ellen staring at her own face in the mirror, made eye contact with Ellen in the mirror, turned around to give Ellen privacy, felt Ellen walk quickly past him, into the hallway, and heard Ellen's door slam shut.

I thought we could either gchat, then edit later, or meet in person and transcribe whatever happens w/o editing (including things like ["long pause"] and ["nervously laughs"]. I think I kind of prefer the 2nd.

So began my interaction with author Tao Lin, a young author known as much for his self-promotional antics as for his several published novels. I wanted to interview Lin about his experiences with a popular image board called 4chan, known for being a

playground for internet trolls and the birthplace of the "hacktivist" collective known as Anonymous. 4chan is a place where thousands of people gather for cheap thrills: porn, gore, and spontaneous collaborative pranks that range from harmlessly goofy to insidiously dangerous. 4chan trolls go after religious cults, white supremacists, scam artists, pedophiles, and animal abusers. They also seem to hate Tao Lin. I wanted to know why.

4chan is a collection of image boards that allows users to anonymously post messages that disappear quickly unless they contain content that inspires others to respond. It is marked by the presence of a geeky, insular cultural currency of internet-borne ephemera which we've now decided to collectively call "memes." For the most part, 4chan's users just want to kill time shooting the shit with other geeks. They talk about anime, mecha, papercraft and other mostly-geeky topics. I've been hanging out on 4chan pretty regularly since 2007 – it's a fascinating Darwinian "meme-pool," from which much of internet culture derives. I wrote a book about 4chan last fall. [1]

Two years ago, 4chan's administrator added a literature board, or, /lit/, to the fifty or so extant forums. It was an immediate personal thrill to see the often puerile tone of 4chan's boards used to describe Dostoyevsky, for instance. The content on the /lit/ board proved what I'd always suspected about 4chan in general – that it's populated by genuinely smart folks who feign stupidity in order to crack each other up. Being on 4chan is a sort of meta-game, a performance art in which everyone tries to be more offensive, funny, shocking, clever, or otherwise fascinating than everyone else in the room.

Still, the /lit/ board demonstrates 4chan's overwhelming geekiness, with sci-fi and fantasy discussion taking up much more of the board's pages than you might see anywhere else. Which is why I was caught off guard when I saw Tao Lin's name referenced there, as opposed to Ray Bradbury or Ayn Rand. According to the board's users, 4chan hates Tao Lin because they claim he uses the board to plug his work, which flies in the face of the site's culture of pure anonymity. They also hate him because he's an NYC hipster artfag.

When /lit/ launched two years ago, Tao Lin was an emerging indie literary icon with a reputation driven by Gawker-fueled haterade. In 2007, Gawker's Emily Gould [3] wrote:

Tao Lin, I know you're reading this. I just want you to know that because of your ill-conceived self-marketing strategy, you have 100% guaranteed that I will never read your damned book with its oh-so-wacky title... Your publicity games aren't a play on fame-seeking or celebrity culture. Actually, you're maybe perhaps the single most irritating person we've ever had to deal with – and you wouldn't believe our in-box. Stop it. Stop it now. And now we will go back to never mentioning you again.

Oh, but how they mentioned him again. And again and again. He badgered them and other media outlets until it worked. Tao eventually became an NYC media darling. Gould and Lin are also besties now, apparently. [4]

How did all this start? Why is Gawker picking on you? Is it because of your success as a young writer?

I emailed them probably like five times over like a year or two before my first two fiction books came out. But like I wanted that. I was happy that happened.

Do you think you'd be where you are today if that buzz hadn't been generated?

Umm, I don't know how big of an effect it had. I don't know some people might view me a lot differently I think. My books, they're like, conventional literary novels and short stories, so without all the internet stuff, a lot of people just view me as a normal literary writer, and that might've helped me in some way.

Would you encourage young writers to let their work speak for itself?

I never advise people on anything. But I think I let my work speak for itself. All that other stuff is its own project. I never respond to reviews saying my book is good or anything. I view negative reviews as another way for more people to find out about the book. So I think it's helpful for that.

Although much of the 4chan experience is built around role-playing, the crowd despises contrived cool. Being geeks, many of 4chan's users are likely kids who were or are currently getting picked on in high school. To them, the internet is a refuge, a place where one's reputation is only as good as his last post. Being good looking, rich, or in this case, a part of an ultra-cool literary elite means nothing on 4chan, and could even count against you if you're foolish enough to hang around there dropping your own name.

Which is why "Go to bed, Tao Lin" is a meme on /lit/. When someone brings up Lin's name, another will inevitably respond with this phrase, which basically means, "We know it's you Tao, doing more viral marketing for your stupid books." I became fascinated by /lit/'s vacillating fascination and hatred of this peculiar author, who would seem so far removed from 4chan geek culture. Despite the differences in environment and focus, 4chan and Lin may have something in common: trolling. It's a different kind of trolling, to be sure, and I believe Lin would cringe at the drawing of such a parallel, but at the heart of it, Lin's public-facing image is thoroughly marked by prankish stunts and apparently (given the self-awareness of the opening quote) put-on awkward-ness that it can only be interpreted as a way to provoke a response, usually something along the lines of, "Is this motherfucker for real?"

How did you first hear about 4chan?

Uhhh, sometime in college, probably 2003 or 2004. Probably just from reading some news thing. I remember looking at it briefly in a computer lab. I think I was looking at /b/ and had like, I don't know it was like, dead babies or something, so I closed it.

Did you continue looking at it semi-regularly?

No. Not until I got Google alerts from people talking about me. Every thread from the beginning, the second or third comment would be like, "Get out of here, Tao." and it wasn't me.

At what point did you start responding to this chatter?

I never really responded. Maybe for like 30% of the threads I'll say something. Like if they're talking about Muumuu house, I'll put a link to Mummu house and say, "Hey, it's Tao, go here."

Tao Lin wrote a book called, *EEEEE EEE EEEE*. He has a blog located at http://hehehehehehehehehehehehehe.tumblr.com/. He can be viewed on YouTube giving a reading in which he repeats the words "the next night we ate whale," ad nauseum for several minutes, provoking his audience to laughter, then confusion, then laughter again. [5] The performance seems designed to test the willingness of his audience to put up with his contrived oddness, like Andy Kaufman reading *The Great Gatsby* in its entirety to a disbelieving audience that showed up for comedy. These and other bizarre publicity stunts have engendered as much love as hate. Bloggers, eager to demonstrate that they are in on the joke, describe Lin as the first author to really figure out how to harness the viral potential of the web, while his detractors see him as just another boring publicity hound whose actual work doesn't stand up to scrutiny from those who are able to look past his trollish antics.

What's different about the chatter on the /lit/ board than some other board? Is it all trollish or is there actually interesting commentary?

[long pause]. I like the tone more, usually.

Is it interesting because it comes from outside a media elite world?

[long pause] I think it's more of a joke. That's what I like reading.

Do you think of yourself as a meme on 4chan?

No.

Do people Photoshop you?

They take images and write stuff on it. There's an image of me and my dad and it says, like, some stereotypical Asian thing about a dad being disappointed in his son. I like that one.

Why do you think you became a known entity on the /lit/ board?

Some of it... some of it's probably because I would write about it on Twitter. Probably cuz of that.

Do you think it has anything to do with some of the information on the internet about you that they might perceive as antagonistic or prankish?

Yeah. I think a lot of what I do is easy to talk about. To make jokes out of. Like almost everything I do that isn't a book is [long pause] has that in mind, to be interesting in that way. So it's just easy for them to talk about me.

I first became aware of the author through *Hipster Runoff*, [6] a pseudonymous cultural criticism blog written satirically in the voice of an achingly self-aware, self-hating hipster who can't bear taking any official stance on any subject without couching his views within ironic scare quotes. The character behind *Hipster Runoff* delights in skewering self-promoters within various creative industries. His most recent target is Elizabeth Grant, a young woman who has similarly parlayed internet vitriol into a successful career under the name Lana del Ray.

Riding a wave of negative feedback, and encouraging its continued churn is nothing new in the arts. Think the aforementioned Andy Kaufman, Steve Albini, or Andy Warhol. Think Salvador Dali walking an anteater around Lower Manhattan on a leash, seemingly oblivious to the shock he's inspiring from every angle. We can agree that he knew what he was doing, right? These guys were patron saints of modern day internet trolling, which we'll broadly define as deriving enjoyment or personal gain from upsetting someone's emotional equilibrium.

Last November *Village Voice* music critic Maura Johnston coined this practice within the music industry "trollgaze," a clever riff on last year's music journo trend in which bloggers devised acrobatic new ways to describe emerging, trendy music genres (chillwave, rapegaze, shitgaze, etc). I'll let her define the term, with some wonderful examples: [7]

2011 has been the year of "trollgaze," a media-agnostic genre name for those pieces of pop culture as designed for maximum Internet attention as they are pieces of art that can stand (or at least wobble) on their own. The ways to get inducted into the trollgaze pantheon are as plentiful as self-congratulatory Lil B retweets; in music alone, they can involve dropping songs chock-full of easy ways to laugh at them (extra points if you're being dead serious about doing so), acting like an entitled punkass brat, complaining about people saying that you're acting like an e.p.b., or somewhat ineptly playing on the already-existent prejudices possessed by critical-mass online audiences, among other things. With so many things these days vying for the masses' increasingly divided attention, though, it's becoming tougher and tougher to gauge whether or not a piece of cultural ephemera is actually trying to double as its social-media strategy.

Basically, this strain of trolling means being outrageously obnoxious and / or odd in order to develop an inscrutable public persona, which ostensibly will lead to increased exposure courtesy of head-scratching and / or facepalming journalists and subsequently, fame and / or fortune. The goal is to leave everyone scrambling to figure out your public-facing image, your actual self, and (last and probably least) your art – and where the three meet and diverge.

When I pitched this piece around, I got the following response back from one editor:

Well, this is an interesting piece... But there's no way to cover Tao Lin without feeding his endlessly ongoing machinations of public relations, so we don't like to do it. Having been the victim of years of his fake emails from "interns" and "friends," I don't have any interest in supporting his gross striving, which I find really offputting (and, to be fair, appropriate for the times). He's a fascinating social experiment, to be sure! But really also just the most craven and I can't even deal with it.

I had initially envisioned this piece as an article about Lin's relationship with 4chan. I wanted to figure out if he really is trolling /lit/ as viral marketing as the board claims, or if he really just happened to achieve memehood on the site through no active engagement of his own. I wanted to see if 4chan had conjured an image of Lin that was based more on hype and lazy readings than reality, and draw parallels to the often silly and unfair way the mainstream media has recently portrayed 4chan's Anonymous, routinely reporting sensationalized linkbait stories about the culture without conducting the slightest bit of fact-checking. I wanted to explore how the internet encourages shallow interpretations of strange and complex phenomena.

When I met Lin for drinks I honestly wasn't sure if he was going to behave like an actual human or some kind of Martian, given his reputation and online persona. Clearly this guy realizes that some people see him as an awkward weirdo, and he seems to enjoys cultivating that image. He must know what he's doing, to some extent. It's possible that he's been so deeply dedicated to his public persona (It's worked out for him so far, I would hardly blame him) that he is at this point oblivious of a distinction between the two.

You said once that you view your microcelebrity like a video game, in which the goal is to have as much fun while racking up points. I think the way people behave on 4chan is like a video game, where they're trying to manipulate the system. Is that similar to what you're trying to do with marketing your personal brand?

[10 second pause] I think I'm just trying to do things that are interesting to me. And to avoid anything that is [long pause] just only promoting something without itself being something that would be interesting even if it wasn't promoting anything. And that makes it so [ten second pause]. The things I do [ten second pause]. I don't know. Can we talk more about the game aspect?

I see the hacking and trolling and pranking like a video game. People start playing a game they're figuring a way to break the boundaries of the system and master it to the point where they've broken the game. That's how people on 4chan treat the internet. Like how they try to find pedophiles and bring them to the attention of law enforcement. They see themselves as heroes in a video game almost. I see similarities with you because you're testing the boundaries of what people will find acceptable and playing with people's preconceived notions. I think you must be aware of what's going to cause rage on 4chan, but also Tumblr and Twitter and elsewhere.

I'm not interested in doing things that are going to intentionally cause outrage or arguments. When I do something [long pause] I don't want what I do to cause a discussion about what's good or bad. [fifteen second pause] I just make an effort not to engage in [long pause] saying controversial things about politics or race or sex or making grandiose statements like "this is the best whatever" or "top ten best whatever" or saying anything's bad to cause a reaction. I try to avoid all those things. But to still do things that will get like, attention.

On the evening of February 20, I went to a reading hosted by Tao Lin featuring mostly young writers from his MuuMuu house collective. When I watched him and a half dozen of his friends on-stage, staring at the floor, picking at their hair, and laughing nervously into the mic, part of me wanted to call them out. But the crowd adored them. With every stutter, every "uh, I lost my place," the crowd clapped for more. The event seemed engineered to satisfy a certain type of beret-wearing NYU student (I counted four). They came to see people so deeply artistic, just overflowing with Imagination and Truth and Beauty, that they can't be bothered to present themselves to the crowd like functioning adults. It's as if these artists want to possess the mystery of the social outcast without having to suffer any actual social ostracism.

But maybe there's something deeper to this contrived faux awkwardness. Maybe it's a defense mechanism. It could be a method of dealing with a legit social anxiety disorder. If I lay all my *[nervous laughs]* and all my *[long pauses]* out there in the open for everyone to see, and preemptively undermine myself, that robs my critics of their ammunition when they try to attack the integrity of my actual work.

My interview with Tao Lin tells us little about what drives him to maybe-troll 4chan nerds or the lit and art publications who write features about him. The interview was at least thirty percent [long pause]. Lin gave me bare responses to many of my questions, and when presented with follow-up questions attempting to wring juice from his stony replies, he responded with yes, *[nervous laughter]* and if I was lucky, *[slightly reworded repetitions]*. Given the way Lin suggested that we frame the interview, I am inclined to believe that Lin wanted it to be this way.

You once said that people think of you as a gimmicky asshole. Where do you think that perception comes from if you're not out there actively trolling?

[fifteen-second pause] Let's just take the example of me selling shares of Richard Yates. I sold six shares for 10% each and made $12,000. That was covered in a lot of places and a lot of places put in their headline that I'd sold shares of a book that I hadn't written yet, but in the blog post I'd said that it was 98 or 95% written. But I knew Gawker and other places would do whatever they needed to seem most outrageous so I just like encouraged, or didn't like make a strong effort to like say, "Actually, this book is almost finished." I think that's typical of coverage of anything. It's just angled to make it seem most outrageous. [10 second pause] I always am in, like, support of the person who's getting shit-talked now, whenever I read anything anywhere pretty much, but that's just because I've been through like so much of it.

When I initially decided to write about Tao Lin I wanted to figure out who is trolling whom among Lin, 4chan, Gawker, Hipster Runoff, and linkbaity mainstream media outlets, and yes, myself. I know this article is going to generate some controversy, so one could argue that I'm trolling Lin, here. And maybe if Lin or other influencers tweet the URL of this article, some of his social capital will rub off on me.

This is how we get attention in 2012 – we're all trolls, trying to upset our audience's emotional equilibrium. We're aiming for some visceral response that drives controversy, eventually leading to increased social standing or financial gain. The internet rewards weirdness. One of meme-centric content aggregator Buzzfeed's eight content categories is "WTF?" We love the internet because it tells us that there's always a freak out there more broken than we are. But standing out in this crowded space requires one to role-play at oddness. We're all so rich and beautiful and educated and fashionable, the only remaining way to differentiate oneself in the status game is to come off as just super real, man. What shall we call it? Awkwave? Weirdgaze?

Lin insists that his motives are pure, that he's not interested in provocation. I'm not sure if I buy this defense. I think his persona is ultimately a reaction against the hyper-self-aware blogosphere and its ironic distance. To be publicly awkward is to reject social norms is to "not give a shit" is to be vulnerable is to be authentic: that ever-elusive ideal of the age. We put ourselves out there, warts and all, desperately hoping that someone will recognize us as real, when really, our awkwardness and hyper-sincerity is just an additional layer of pretense.

I genuinely like Tao Lin. He's an awfully nice and polite guy. His Twitter is sometimes hilarious. I think his writing is interesting and occasionally even genius. He's had nice things to say about my writing. Sometimes he even "likes" my Tumblr posts. This observation isn't directed solely at him, rather a broader trend among young creatives. I'm not trying to pick on Lin – maybe he actually does suffer from social anxiety disorder. I'm using him as a lens through which to analyze this widespread phenomenon. I'm certainly not suggesting, when accusing him of trolling, that Lin is doing anything mean, like kind of troll who writes, "lol someone should rape that slut" on some poor 11-year old's YouTube video.

But with MuuMuu house, Lin seems to be training a growing generation of otherwise bright writers and artists to troll for press (or are we to buy any narrative that describes publishing a photo of a famous editor's semen on one's face as something other than a naked publicity grab exchanging female sexual self-sabotage for mad page views?). And I can't help but feel like this is a road to artistic irrelevance. My generation is one that appears to be devoting tremendous amounts of creative energy into the development of a personal brand at the expense of its artistic production. I wish Lin and his acolytes would let their talent speak for itself, without the spectacle of eccentricity. This approach might not generate as much hype, but perhaps man cannot live on buzz alone.

During our interview, I fielded some questions from /lit/ and asked Lin to respond.

"Ask him how he has overcome his autism."
I really like the autism meme. It's really funny.

"Is his next novel about 4chan?"
No. Though I had an idea to title it 4chan as a complete *non sequitur.*

"Ask him why he just doesn't come out and say: 'Hey /lit/! Tao here! Let's talk about books!' and instead has made no less than a thousand threads here more along the lines of: 'heehee no one knows it's me but if I keep posting it I'll be the Jeff Mangum of /lit/ [7] heehee, hey Megan Boyle [8] you make threads too and you too intern heeheehee I'm a fucking faggot.'"
[nervous laughter]

First published on Rhizome on March 27, 2012. Available online at
http://rhizome.org/editorial/2012/mar/27/tao-lin/.

COLE STRYKER (http://colestryker.com/) writes mostly about the Web and helps
agencies and brands make their stuff go viral through media strategy at Giant Media.
He is the author of Epic Win for Anonymous: How 4chan's Army Conquered the Web
and Hacking the Future, both published in 2011. The first is about the hacktivist group
Anonymous and the memetic culture from which it spawned. The second presents a
broader history of anonymity as a social construct. He is currently working on a third
book about the "Deep Web."

Notes

[1] Cole Stryker, *Epic Win for Anonymous: How 4chan's Army Conquered the
Web*, Overlook, 2011.
[2] Cf. Joanne McNeil, "Cole Stryker, Author of 'Epic Win for Anonymous' on
Interior Semiotics, Context Collapse, and 'You Rage You Lose'", in *Rhizome*,
September 12, 2011, online at http://rhizome.org/editorial/2011/sep/12/cole-
stryker-epic-win/.
[3] Emily Gould, "Now We Also Hate Miranda July", in *Gawker*, June 27, 2007,
online at http://gawker.com/272734/now-we-also-hate-miranda-july.
[4] Cf. Episode 15 of the "internet cooking show" Cooking the Books, hosted
by Emily Gould, in which she invites famous authors into her kitchen to make
food inspired by their books. The video is available online at
www.youtube.com/watch?v=d2BJSV8Q1Yw.
[5] Cf. www.youtube.com/watch?v=QjcOK2T0IPo.
[6] Cf. http://www.hipsterrunoff.com/tag/tao-lin.
[7] The former singer of indie rock band Neutral Milk Hotel is a meme on
4chan's music board /mu/, signifying hipster weirdness.
[2] Tao's wife.

274

275

LINK Editions

http://editions.linkartcenter.eu/

Clouds

Domenico Quaranta, *In Your Computer*, 2011
Valentina Tanni, *Random*, 2011
Gene McHugh, *Post Internet*, 2011
Brad Troemel, *Peer Pressure*, 2011
Kevin Bewersdorf, *Spirit Surfing*, 2012
Mathias Jansson, *Everything I shoot Is Art*, 2012
Joanne McNeil (Ed.), *Best of Rhizome 2012*, 2013

Catalogues

Collect the WWWorld. The Artist as Archivist in the Internet Age, 2011. Exhibition Catalogue. Edited by Domenico Quaranta, with texts by Josephine Bosma, Gene McHugh, Joanne McNeil, Domenico Quaranta
Gazira Babeli, 2011. Exhibition catalogue. Edited by Domenico Quaranta, with texts by Mario Gerosa, Patrick Lichty, Domenico Quaranta, Alan Sondheim.
Holy Fire. Art of the Digital Age, 2011. Exhibition catalogue. Edited by Yves Bernard, Domenico Quaranta.

In My Computer

Miltos Manetas, *In My Computer # 1*, 2011
Ryan Trecartin, *Ryan's Web 1.0. A Lossless Fall*, 2012

LINK Editions is a publishing initiative of the **LINK Center for the Arts of the Information Age**. LINK Editions uses the print on demand approach to create an accessible, dynamic series of essays and pamphlets, but also tutorials, study notes and conference proceedings connected to its educational activities.